How to Shape Your Child's Education

How to Shape Your Child's Education

Combine the power of the home, the school, and peers to help your child thrive in school.

Cliff Schimmels

LIFEJOURNEY
BOOKS

David C. Cook Publishing Co.
Elgin, Illinois   Weston, Ontario

LifeJourney Books is an imprint of David C. Cook Publishing Co.
David C. Cook Publishing Co., Elgin, Illinois 60120
David C. Cook Publishing Co., Weston, Ontario

HOW TO SHAPE YOUR CHILD'S EDUCATION
(Also published as *How to Help Your Child Survive and Thrive in Public School*)
© 1989 Cliff Schimmels

Cover design by Russ Peterson
Book design by April Frost
Back cover photo by Ron Ericksen Photography

First printing, 1989
Printed in the United States of America
93 92 91 90 89 5 4 3 2 1

Schimmels, Cliff.
      How to Shape Your Child's Education
        1. Education, Elementary—United States. 2. Child
      rearing—United States. 3. Home and school—United
      States. I. Title.
LB 1555.S25 1989 372.973—dc19
ISBN 1-55513-069-0   89-762
                          CIP

CONTENTS

1

Who Owns Your Child?

At twenty-six years of age, I was a football genius. I knew I was a genius because I had just persuaded a school board in a small town in western Kansas to employ me as head football coach. Early in August I moved to that town, carrying with me all my prized possessions: my young family, my frequently read Darrel Royal football book, an organized system of X's and O's that I had pieced together from notes on coffee shop napkins, and my dreams.

Dreams I had in abundance, and I cherished each one dearly. Secretly but vividly I had planned the next two decades. I had already practiced my acceptance speech for the time when I would be chosen the town's "Man of the Year." I had rehearsed the humbleness required to shake hands with an opposing coach whom I had just beaten by four touchdowns. I had lost a few pounds so I wouldn't be such a load when my players raised me to their shoulders and carried me off the field. I was ready to coach.

About a week before the first practice, I was dreaming and planning in my office when the principal called to announce the father of a player.

The man walked in and sat down as if he owned the place—taxpayers sometimes act that way. "You the new football coach?" he asked.

"Yes, sir." I don't think he detected the trembling in my voice.

"What are you going to do here?"

That was a question I could get into. "Well, I'm going to implement a Wing T offense with a man in motion and a flip-flop line. We'll have a lot of power on the corners, but we'll still be able to get three receivers out quick." I was just getting warmed up as he interrupted.

"Is that all?"

Surmising that he was not offense-minded, I took a new twist.

"No, not at all. I'm going to put in the stack-4 defense with a lot of stunting. As far as I know, no one in the area is running such a defense, so we should really have surprise on our side."

He interrupted again. "Anything else?"

I had about exhausted my repertoire of dreams and plans, so I dug a little deeper. "Well, I do have a very elaborate off-season program planned. We combine running, weights, and isometrics, and spend a lot of time just thinking football."

"Yeah?"

"Well, and I do intend to teach the young men a lot about personal integrity and sportsmanship and playing the game with a positive attitude to maximize the fun aspect of good, hard-nosed football."

"I just hope you can get my kid to cut his hair. I've tried everything, and he refuses to do it."

With that, my guest got up and walked out.

Your Child or the School's?

In those few minutes, I learned the most important lesson I have learned in more than twenty years in the dual professions of teacher and parent. As I sat in that football office with the tips of my ears the color of pickled beets, I realized that perhaps parents and school people ought to get together more often. I learned that I could never become a very effective teacher until I had some sense of what was happening to the child at home. I also learned that I could never become a very effective parent until I understood what was happening to the child at school.

Who is to blame for the unfortunate gap that too often exists between these two agencies? We could start with all the young coaches and teachers who begin their professions with so much idealism that sometimes they refuse to see everyday, practical concerns and possible solutions. Or we could blame the parents for their willingness to pass off parental responsibility to an outside agency. But fixing blame is a hard task. Like the six blind men of Indostan who went to see the elephant, both parents and teachers can be partly in the right yet entirely in the wrong.

Young teachers do have a right to be idealistic, to think they can change the world, alter community direction, and make rain come during droughts. And parents do have a right to expect something to happen in the schools.

But as educators and parents spend their time pointing accusing fingers and wondering what each can expect from the other, there lurks in the wings the most important character in this dramatic conflict: that long-haired football player. Somebody has to worry about him—his physical, emotional, spiritual, and moral needs.

Whom are you willing to trust with the authority to tell *your* child to cut his hair? Who is going to provide the information, the knowledge, the understanding, the love, the commitment, the discipline, and the example needed to enable your child to grow into the personhood for which God has ordained him?

Somebody has to provide those things, and has to provide them in such a way that your child can accept them. There have never been many guarantees in child rearing. There are even fewer now. The secret to success is hidden somewhere in how the parents and the school can coordinate their efforts so that the child can sort through the messages and find some direction. That is what this book is about.

The Biblical Mandate

More than 3,000 years ago God established some principles that He thought were important, and He designated an institution to oversee and perpetuate those principles. Our culture is still in existence because of the institution that has faithfully passed along those guidelines throughout the generations. What is the institution with such a holy and responsible task? Is it a great church? A system of government? An international communication system? No. For a task so important, God ordained the institution of parenthood.

In the Old Testament Book of Deuteronomy, God said, through the voice of Moses, "These words, which I am commanding you today, shall be on your heart; and you shall teach them diligently to your sons and shall talk of them when you sit in your house and when you walk by the way and when you lie down and when you rise up" (Deuteronomy 6:6-7).

Modern parents might protest that the injunction should be generalized, that God is suggesting only that the older generation should teach the younger. But that is not the way the ancient Israelite read the mandate, and that is not the way the apostle Paul reaffirmed it in his Epistles.

Let me make some assumptions about you and your relationship to the mandate.

1. *Your child is the most precious possession you have, and you realize this.*

By using the word *possession,* I do not mean to put the child on the level of a new pair of shoes or a used station wagon. I don't even mean that you put your child on the level of a profession or a philosophy of life or a set of beliefs.

But during your lifetime you are going to invest your energy, time, creative wisdom, judgment, decisions, and moral integrity in a variety of projects and possessions. Among those—job, house, bank account, or whatever—the only one which is going to survive you and represent you as a significant force in this world after you have left it is your child. His rearing deserves some attention.

2. *You really do want the school to be successful in relating to your child's needs.*

Don't be too shocked by that statement. After several years of counseling with parents and students, I have concluded that some people are actually hoping the school will fail. I guess they like saying, "I told you so."

Examine yourself; see if you can honestly trust the school and are willing to give it the credit for its role in the positive development of your child. Are you prepared to say, "I really like the way the coach got my son to cut his hair"? Are you prepared to admit, "The teacher succeeded where I failed"? It takes some parental nobility to admit this, but I assume that you are a noble person.

3. *You are willing (perhaps even excited) to accept your full responsibility in the education of your own child.*

One of the conveniences of living in the posteverything age is that we have some agency to take care of every phase of human living; more importantly, we have someone to blame for failure in any phase. If I am not as handsome as Burt Reynolds, it's my barber's fault. If I have a heart attack, it's my doctor's fault. If the automobile doesn't operate efficiently, it's the mechanic's fault. If my child doesn't know how to read or gets pregnant or in any way offends her parentage, it's the school's fault.

In spite of how good or bad schools may be or can be or should be, the frightening truth is that you have as much responsibility as anyone in educating your child. I am assuming that you want your child to read, to write, to score well on standardized tests, and to demonstrate other indications of having been educated. But I am also assuming that you are willing to make some sacrifices of your own time and talent to see that this happens.

With the rise in private and Christian schools in recent years, many parents have been given more choice in where their children attend school. It is good that parents should have this choice, and it is also good that public schools do not have a monopoly on children's education. But the very existence of this choice places an unusual responsibility on parents. They now must know enough about the whole, wonderful process of education to be able to make a wise decision.

School, Family, and Friends

In the first section of this book, I will report my observations of schools, gathered from twenty years in various teaching assignments. I will help you develop some criteria, based on these observations, for judging the soundness of a school, and I will enumerate in clear terms where the school—any school, your child's school—is inadequate or helpless and must have your support.

The second section is dedicated to the purpose of helping you think about how your family works as an educational agent in your child's life. Every day at three-thirty when the school's dismissal bell rings, it is time for a sometimes faltering, nebulous institution called the family to assume its direct responsibility for the education of the child. Since we adults are by age the mature force in our families, we are the ones who need to think about doing it right.

The thesis of the third section of this book is that the peer group is a powerful influence in the lives of most young people. This whole issue of peer pressure requires diligent, wise, judicial guidance and sincere prayer. It is here that the parents and the school have mutual concerns and frustrations. It is here that the school and parents must work together and must depend on each other.

The information in this part of the book is largely based on the mistakes I have seen parents make, and I find that admission frightening. But if we have to learn difficult lessons from mistakes, I would prefer to learn them by observation rather than by direct experience.

If you are a parent, God has entrusted you with a rare privilege, the privilege of directing a life through its formative and crucial period. Like any other important task, there is always a risk. There are various powers or influences that come together in that one single life: the school, the family, the peers. It is my belief that one of the important roles of the parent is to see that those powers speak as one unified voice.

Yes, sir. What style would you like your child's hair to be?

Homework Assignments for Parents

1. How diligent have you been so far in teaching your child the things you want him to know? How might you need to adapt your level of involvement at this point in his life?

2. How do you feel about your child's school? Are you leaving certain things to the school that you should be doing? Do you ever resent seeing the school succeed in some area where you have failed?

3. Do you take full responsibility for your child's development? Or do you tend to blame the school in certain areas? Think of some specific examples.

SECTION 1: THE POWER OF THE SCHOOL SYSTEM

2

The Myth of the "School System"

Exhibit A. The third-grade students were reading all about planets in their *Weekly Readers*. Since there were various levels of reading competence in the room, the teacher walked quietly about during the silent time. Armed with gentleness and a quick smile, he would stop and help a student through a more difficult passage. Finally, all students had completed the reading and were sitting quietly with their readers folded on their desk-tops.

The teacher, still mobile and still graciously armed, began to ask questions. At first, only the hands of the brighter, more aggressive students flew to the air of recognition; but soon, the sequence of questions built to a climax as more students began to plead for an opportunity to respond. The teacher went slowly, but with enthusiasm. Each student's answer was rewarded with a comment, a smile, and perhaps an added thought. If a student wanted to add to an answer from one of his colleagues or wanted to ask an additional question, he was given the time and the climate to conclude his investigation. Each child in the room volunteered some kind of oral participation during the lesson.

Time flew quickly. At the conclusion those students could name and spell the planets, place them in their order from the sun, explain their rotation, recite several characteristics about each, and explain the meaning of days and years on earth.

When they were finished, the teacher thanked them for their response and rewarded each with a Mars bar.

Exhibit B. The algebra class was stumped. The student had just written his problem on the chalkboard. He had shown all the necessary steps toward solution and had circled the number which represented the right answer.

The teacher asked, "Is that the right answer?"

"Yes," the student responded.

The teacher furrowed his brow as if in thought and then asked, "If that is the right answer, what does it mean?"

The student was slightly irritated. "What kind of question is that? I found the right answer; what do you mean, 'What does the right answer mean?' "

The teacher disarmed him with a grin, but continued the questioning. "Students, there are many problems in life which may have a right answer, but just finding it is not good enough. Even though we discover the right answer to the algebra question, we must know *why* it is the right answer. Now, who can help him out? What does it mean to us that this is the right answer?"

The room was filled with a busy silence. Eyes narrowed as they studied the writing on the board and mouths curled into inquisitiveness. Twenty-nine minds focused on the question, *What is the meaning of the right answer?* The teacher waited patiently for what might have seemed too long for a less-informed educator.

Finally, one student offered a possibility. With gentleness but a commitment to the discovery of meaning, the teacher began the questioning anew. Throughout the rest of the period, the students applied the test of "why" to their right solutions. They confirmed algebraic equations, they pursued mathematical theories, and they pondered the meaning of *meaning*. During that time, there were no discipline problems, no horseplay, no harsh words, and no lack of interest.

Exhibit C. The classroom was in chaos. When the bell rang, the students wandered in, listlessly and casually. Some made it before the tardy bell, but most didn't. The history teacher sat in the front of the room at his desk and called the roll without looking up. After each name was called, a student answered with a perfunctory "here." In a few isolated cases, the "here's" came weakly, after a long silence, accompanied by nervous giggling which certified that it was bogus.

Still sitting, the teacher taught for the day. "Okay. Read the next chapter in your book and answer the questions at the end. We are going to have a test on it Friday."

Someone asked, not completely interested, "Which chapter is it?"

Another student asked, "Do we have to hand in the questions?"

"If you want a grade for them, you do."

Again, a student asked, "Are we going to get back the questions we handed in last week?"

"Yes," the teacher answered.

"When?" It was more of a dare than a question.

"When I get them graded; that's when. What do you people think I am, anyway? I have things to do, too. Now shut up and get to work on the next chapter."

With that, the teacher picked up the sports magazine from his desk and proceeded to flip through it, pausing occasionally to check the progress of the class through the vantage point of his feet resting on the desk-top.

A group of boys congregated in one back corner, watching a student carve a dirty word on the desk, talking and laughing coarsely. A small group of girls occupied the other back corner and practiced the art of cosmetics—brushing hair, painting nails, dabbing eye makeup. Two young men sat in the middle of the room and played a computer game. Another student read the newspaper. A few students, scattered throughout the room, silently read the chapter assigned.

Teacher: The Key to the School Experience

Let me assure you that these stories are true. In a one-week period, I observed each one, all in the same district—the latter two in the same building.

What is the point? Simple. Considering the diversity in approaches and in enthusiasm which individual teachers bring to their classrooms, it is rather difficult to make any generalizations about the school system. For the student, the classroom teacher is the school system.

In actual practice, it is a mistake to think of school in terms of a system. I realize the natural tendency to think that way. It is comfortable, particularly if one aspires to be a reformer. It is easy and safe to criticize a system. A system is impersonal. You can blame the system for all your miseries, yet never be faced with the threat of confrontation. No one is the system, so you can even criticize the system to the man in charge without ruffling feelings.

Since the federal constitution is silent about the subject of education, the process becomes, by implication of omission, one of the states' rights under the Tenth Amendment. Thus, there are at least fifty different school systems in the United States. But in each state there are districts—more than 16,000 across the nation—with individual boards, individual needs, individual moods, and individual values; so each district becomes a system. Within each district, each building has a unique personality, a spirit or attitude that makes it a system unto itself. And within each building, each classroom teacher has an individual style, likes and dislikes, specific emphases, a manner of response, a special approach to the art of living.

For your child, the system of education in the United States is defined by what happens in *one classroom*. If that teacher is good, or your child perceives the teacher to be good, then the educational system is good. If that teacher is inadequate and insensitive, then the educational system is bad. It is quite possible for a specific student to go through a school system, from kindergarten to high school graduation, and get an excellent education because he or she, by chance, was always placed in the right classroom. It is also possible that a student could go that same route and never have a really good teacher.

Each year, I ask more than 100 college seniors why they chose their particular college major (which in many instances is the same as choosing a lifetime profession). More than 90 percent of them give the same answer, "When I was in elementary school [or high school], I had a good teacher in that field." One chance meeting in the schooling process, and an entire life is given direction!

Teacher: A Constant in a Sea of Change

For convenience, educators frequently divide the schooling process into three categorical levels: the principle level, the policy level, and the practice level.

During my twenty years in the educational profession, I have seen changes in the *principles* upon which school officials base decisions. I have seen a greater emphasis on the doctrine of separation of church and state in Supreme Court cases. I have seen restrictions and limitations on school finances. I have seen new attitudes and laws regarding minorities. I have seen changes in course requirements and stiffer teacher-certification standards. For the crusader who carried the cause, each change in principle represented a major achievement, a worthy accomplishment which followed months, perhaps years, of active battle. Yet, in spite of all those efforts, for most children, school is about the same as it was before the battles were won.

During my years in teaching, I have also seen changes in educational *policies*. I have seen the coming and going of dress and hair codes. I have seen the construction and destruction of high school smoking areas. I have seen new emphasis on courses in drugs, economics, values, and driver's education. I have seen an increasing trend to restrict corporal punishment. Yet, school still goes on much as it did 200 years ago.

I have seen changes in educational *practices and programs*. I have seen the modular schedule come and go. I watched the rise and fall of the open classroom. I have heard the proponents and opponents of individual instruction, bicultural education, mainstreaming vocational education, and gifted education. Yet, not all that much has changed.

Despite all the principles, all the policies, and all the programs, the teacher remains the dominant constant in all educational endeavors. Despite all our technology and science, the teaching-learning process is still primarily a human activity. A few highly motivated learners may get some isolated lessons from machines or books, but most of us know most of what we know because someone taught us.

It makes good rhetoric to attack the system, but for the most part the effort is more ambitious than effective. Any real change in the quality of a child's education will begin and be completed not in the United States Congress or in the state capital or in the school board meeting, but in the heart and mind of the *individual teacher.*

The Teacher and the System

Even teachers like to believe in "the system." In most cases, the individual teacher is the key to a successful educational experience and to educational progress. The limits to creativity are in the mind of that teacher in that classroom. Yet, a large percentage will argue vehemently that there is indeed a system and that it prevents them from being as good as they should be. The teachers themselves are the first people who need to understand the guerrilla nature of schools.

Don't get me wrong. I know there are some limitations, restrictions, and rules. I have bumped against a few of these myself from time to time. But there are no rules that demand that any teacher be lazy, rude, unimaginative, or ineffective. These are characteristics of teachers and not characteristics of a system.

When I was a high school principal, we used a standard form for teachers to notify parents if a student was in danger of failing a class. The forms had to go out at least four weeks before the final grading. One day, an algebra teacher came in and asked for sixty forms. Since that represented about seventy-five percent of his student load, I decided to check into the problem.

"Yes," he told me, "they are, in fact, failing algebra."

"But what's the problem? Are they lazy?"

"No," he replied. "They can't do algebra because they can't do simple arithmetic. They can't multiply and divide."

At that particular time in educational history, the report didn't surprise me. Those students had spent their first few years in school during a period of mathematical philosophy which suggested that a child could do calculus before he learned to multiply. Thus, many children didn't learn to multiply.

I thought the solution seemed simple, so I mustered up my best fatherly image, walked around to his side of my desk in an effort to dethrone myself, took a casual pose, and offered some words of great pedagogical wisdom gathered from decades of varied classroom experience. "Why don't you teach them to multiply?"

"But," he answered too quickly, "if I did that, I wouldn't be able to teach algebra."

"Are they learning algebra now?"

"No. Most of them aren't, at least."

"Why not?" This was beginning to sound like a Socratic dialogue.

"Because they can't multiply and divide."

"Well, teach them."

"That takes time."

"Sure it does."

"But then I wouldn't get through the book."

"Who says you've got to get through the book?"

"The principal."

I had him there, I realized—*I* was the principal. "No. My recommendation is for you to begin where they are, with work they can do, and proceed from there."

"But," he retorted, "if I did that, I wouldn't be teaching algebra, and that is what I am getting paid to do."

With that, he stormed back to his room and spent the next six months teaching algebra, while I spent those six months trying to explain to parents why their children weren't learning algebra.

That teacher wasn't bitter. He just had a mistaken notion of his task, and he serves as an illustration of the dangers of thinking in terms of a system. In that situation, the system said to teach algebra to freshmen, regardless of individual differences, unique problems, or special needs. The only person who had the power to correct the inaccurate order was the teacher, and he refused to do so. A new policy wouldn't have done much good. A court order wouldn't have changed things that much. Change had to begin in the attitude of that teacher.

I visit scores of different school buildings every year. On those visits I see a variety of funny designs and hear about a catalog of funny rules. But in every building I have ever visited, there are always teachers who are doing a good job of relating to students and are teaching young people the content of effective and efficient living. *The individual classroom teacher is still the biggest single issue in determining school excellence in this country.*

So we are now back to where we started in this chapter. If you are interested in rallying around noble causes, getting your name in the paper, and winning battles against an anonymous system, you probably won't find much help in this book. But if you are sincerely interested in helping your child survive and perhaps even thrive in this schooling ordeal, and if you are willing to agree that the teacher represents the system to your child, then I think the next three chapters may offer some help and hope.

Homework Assignments for Parents

1. How well does your child like his teacher(s)? Why does he feel the way he does about the teacher?

2. If your child has a teacher he doesn't like, what things can you do to prevent him from identifying the one unliked teacher as typical of the school system?

3. Do you understand why your child's teacher teaches the way he does (even if you don't agree with his teaching style)? Can the teacher recommend to you any educational philosophy books to support his approach?

All Kinds of Teachers

B riar Common Elementary School is loca-
ted in a moderately prosperous suburb in
any American city. The district has not
had unusual financial problems. There are four
sections of the sixth grade at Briar Common, with
approximately twenty-five students per section.

The following are sketches of the four sixth-
grade teachers. Read the sketches carefully, then
respond to the directions which follow.

Mr. Sam Kinner

When Mr. Kinner earned his master's degree
in the early 1970's, he became immersed in the
instructional objectives approach to teaching.
Since then, he has developed a comprehensive,
competency-based curriculum, and he uses
individualized instruction. For every unit, he has
prepared a packet of objectives, readings, and
activities. The objectives tell the students exactly
what is expected of them.

For example: "By the end of this unit, the students will be able to construct a friendly letter with no more than three mechanical errors." "By the end of this unit, the student will be able to identify on a map all the countries of South America." The readings provide the necessary information, and the activities specify the practice needed to achieve the objective.

At the beginning of each unit, Mr. Kinner distributes the packets to the students, who then sit at their desks and complete the packets. Some units can be completed in one or two days, but frequently units take as long as a week or more.

Mr. Kinner spends most of his time checking student progress, encouraging individuals, and administering progress tests. In his class, efficiency is the key. Since the objectives are clearly written, the students know what they must do. Grades are given fairly and objectively. Since the students work individually on the packets, desks are arranged to minimize distraction.

Miss Sally Simon

Miss Simon is a fun teacher. She understands children and has had lots of classes in interpersonal relations, communication skills, role-playing, and transactional analysis. She believes that students should learn to express themselves, to formulate values, and to think.

One of the high spots of each day is the class meeting. During this period the students sit in a circle, and each expresses his or her moods and feelings. This really gets the students ready for the day. It teaches them to be honest with themselves and with others. Some days the class meeting gets so exciting that it might last most of the morning.

Miss Simon also believes that students need to be encouraged to be creative, so the class spends a lot of time reading and writing poetry and performing improvisational dramas. Almost any lesson—history, science, math—can be made interesting and relevant.

Most of the time the desks are pushed out of the way, so the students can sit in circles on the floor or can act out their dramas. Sometimes visitors get the idea that Miss Simon's classes are disorderly and loud, but she says students must be active to learn.

Mrs. Constance Smith

Last year Mrs. Smith was named District Teacher of the Year. The award was particularly appropriate because she was also celebrating her twenty-fifth year in the district. In fact, she has been a sixth-grade teacher in the same classroom for all those twenty-five years. By now, she and her class are a legend.

Students know what to expect in Mrs. Smith's class. They will have to know the states and capitals, all the presidents in order, the countries of South America, the books of the Bible (she still insists on this, and so far no one has protested), and how to divide and multiply whole numbers and fractions. In her class the students will diagram sentences, write frequent reports, and work difficult math problems. There will be homework almost every night.

There aren't many distractions in her class. She doesn't like noise, and students quickly learn when to speak and when not to. The desks are in straight rows.

The bulletin boards are really good because Mrs. Smith spends a lot of money for instructional posters. The chalkboard is always clean. The bookcases are neat. (If the janitors had a vote, they would make Mrs. Smith the District Teacher of the Year every year.)

Despite her success and her recognition, Mrs. Smith doesn't seem as happy as she used to be.

Mr. Don Huey

Mr. Huey is a busy teacher who runs a busy class. He is committed to one educational principle—students must be active. He manages this by what he calls the problem-solving method.

Mr. Huey's day is not divided into blocks of time for arithmetic, history, science, reading, and so on. Instead, he gives the students some kind of a problem which demands that they use a wide range of skills and knowledge to solve. The students use these skills in solving the problems. Most of the time they work in groups, and frequently they are out of the classroom—in the resource center, on the playground, or even downtown in the museums.

Mr. Huey calls himself "a director of learning" rather than a teacher. He spends most of his time discussing progress with one of the groups. He begins sentences with, "Have you considered . . . ?" or "Are you sure . . . ?" or "What do you think . . . ?"

The furniture in the classroom seems disarranged, but it doesn't make much difference. The students never use it anyhow.

Mr. Huey is really a popular teacher, except sometimes with the principal, who thinks Mr. Huey wants to take too many field trips.

Ranking Your Preferences

Now, imagine that you are the parent of an eleven year old who is preparing to enter sixth grade at Briar Common Elementary School. Based on your present knowledge and philosophy of schools, rank the four teachers according to how you would choose them for your child.

_3_ Mr. Sam Kinner

_4_ Miss Sally Simon

_1_ Mrs. Constance Smith

_2_ Mr. Don Huey

Now just for fun, rank the four teachers according to how you would choose them if you were the eleven-year-old student.

_4_ Mr. Sam Kinner

_2_ Miss Sally Simon

_3_ Mrs. Constance Smith

_1_ Mr. Don Huey

How did you do on your test? If you found it easy, I commend you. That means that you have strong opinions about the educational process and that you are prepared to handle some of the decisions which are actually being forced upon some parents by legislation and procedure.

For example, the federal special-education law, Public Law 94-142, requires that parents of special-education students attend and participate in all committee meetings, called staffing, where an individual child's eduction is discussed. Since this requirement is receiving favorable reports, it could soon extend to nearly every child in school, and all parents could find themselves making decisions similar to those you just made.

If you found the test difficult, I identify with you. As a parent (even with all my experience in the field of schools), I find the test hard. For one thing, all those teachers are good at what they are doing. There is no clear-cut case of incompetence here; we are not choosing between good and bad or right or wrong.

These four persons are dedicated teachers who still believe that children are worth the efforts of hard work, that the system can tolerate inventive teaching, and that schooling makes a difference. When you ranked those teachers, you were actually doing the work of educational philosophy. (Of course, these four do not exhaust all the possible educational philosophies swarming about; I have oversimplified for the sake of illustration.)

It is important for you to understand what mental processes and what personal biases you were using when you ranked those teachers. You probably approached the decisions from one of two directions, and the direction you used indicates something about what you think is important to education.

The first direction would be the *practical approach*. If you think this way, you probably said, "I know what I want my children to learn and I know which of these four teachers will get the job done." You might have based your decision on past experience ("*I* know how *I* learned") or you might have based your decision on a feeling of which teacher is most likely to achieve the results you find desirable. All this is practical. You make educational choices based on what works.

The second direction is the more *world-viewish* one. You might have made your decision based on such questions as: What is the implied nature of man at work here? In this person's class, what is the basis of knowledge? Who decides what should be learned? What is learning?

Since there is merit in both the practical and the world-view approach, some combination of the two probably offers the best way for us to evaluate these four teachers. We do need to know what kind of immediate results a particular teacher is going to get, but it is also important to know what those results mean and why we want those results for our children.

Why do you want your child to score well on standardized tests, to be able read when he is six, to multiply, to be reactive, to have a good self-image? I really mean these as more than rhetorical questions. I think all thoughtful parents must at some time back away from their children and the immediate situation and ask what all this means.

What do you want for your child today? Next year? Twenty years from now? Based on that, what kind of teacher does your child need? Which of the four is right, not only for your educational expectations, but also for your child's personality and peculiar learning needs?

Actually, the descriptions themselves are a bit deceptive. On the surface, we get a glimpse of what is happening in four different classrooms, but there is more at work here. To understand fully what is happening to your child, you must look beyond the content, the seating arrangement, and the classroom activities to see what is below the surface, below the descriptions.

The Hidden Curriculum

In recent years we have been warned: beware of the hidden curriculum. The implication of the warning and the warners is that there are some very important lessons hidden within the *way* we do things as well as what we actually do. If, these warners say, we are going to make important decisions about education, we must recognize what is being taught *accidentally* as well as intentionally.

Those people may have a point. As adults, we may find that we have strongly developed habits and attitudes that we can't remember learning. For example, I have always considered myself a nonchauvinistic guy. I have been persuasive in convincing certain high school females that they should be doctors instead of nurses and lawyers instead of secretaries. I am proud of my record. Yet, the other day I drove into a gas station, and a young lady came out to service my car.

Well, I'm not *that* broad-minded. There are still some things which are sacred to masculinity, and my car is one of them. Not only did I not trust my machine to that female mind, but I was also embarrassed to stand there and let this girl do men's work. I cowered on the other side of the auto, walked around as if I were a stranger there, read all the labels in the pop machine, and hid in the men's room for about ten minutes.

Now, I am confused. I don't know how to handle my attitudes toward male supremacy. I have consciously and rationally dealt with the major issues. But suddenly I find that somewhere in my past, completely without my will and without my knowledge, I have learned some very strong attitudes toward sex roles. When did it creep in? I don't know. I never had a lesson in it. I never read a book or saw a film about it. But somewhere I learned never to trust cars to women. That is hidden curriculum.

In his book, *The Abolition of Man,* C. S. Lewis talks about an innocent-looking grammar text. Yet, the approach the authors take toward language is not grammar but ethics, philosophy. Lewis makes the point that ten years hence, the students will take a side in an argument without ever realizing how they developed their position.

Everything the teacher does in the classroom teaches your child something. Every book your child reads teaches him something, both in bold print and between the lines. Every television program, every statement and action you make, every newspaper story your child reads—all blend together and have some effect in shaping that wonderful and mysteriously beautiful thing called your child's mind.

The purpose of this chapter is to help you detect and evaluate the hidden curriculum inherent in a teacher's approach to teaching. But rather than doing the work of investigation for you, I am going to dwell on the technique, to provide you with a method of investigation. Then, if you ever have to make real decisions similar to those you made at the beginning of the chapter, you will have a framework from which to operate. And even if you are not asked to choose which teacher your child has, you will at least be able to understand and help him deal with the hidden lessons he is receiving.

Let's look again at the four teachers. Although each represents a certain philosophical school which comes complete with a polysyllabic title, the labels are generalizations which might get in the way of real investigation, so we will ignore those.

Mr. Kinner's Hidden Curriculum

For centuries, some educators have claimed that the value of schools is to teach children how to be social beings, how to get along with their peers, and how to get along in society when school is finished. But Mr. Kinner does not define education as the process of socialization. That is probably the most distinguishing thing about him.

I don't mean to imply that there is no socialization in Mr. Kinner's class, but it is not the key lesson. For him, the real purpose of schools is to master the written material. The lessons are on paper, not within people. A child's task is to take this written material, study it, and bring it back to the conscious level when it is demanded.

If you look deeply enough into this, you will get an ever-so-small hint that a child and a dog are different only in the child's ability to read. You could use the same principles to train the dog. Decide what you want him to do, create the training sessions with repetition and feedback, and give him a biscuit when he performs.

Of course, reading is absolutely essential in this classroom. If the student doesn't know how to read well, he probably won't like the class much and he won't do well. Perhaps Mr. Kinner will make some provisions for his slower readers, but the emphasis is still there. Students who read quickly will finish faster, so they will probably be encouraged to do more work. The slower readers will struggle to cover the minimum.

Students in Mr. Kinner's class will need to be self-motivated. If they are not interested in learning the material, they could easily whittle every cumulus cloud in the sky into dragons and serpents and heroes, and rarely get to the task. Of course, Mr Kinner has built in some rewards for those who complete their work, but those rewards must be more valuable than mentally whittled cloud dragons if they are going to be of much use.

Students who are particularly well suited for this class are people whose psychological makeup demands organization and direction. They do their best work when the route is clearly defined. These people would function well here because there is direction and little interference.

Of the four teachers discussed, Mr. Kinner would probably do the best job of preparing students to excel on standardized tests. So, if your educational goal for your child is a good score on the SAT or ACT tests, then you would have done well to choose Mr. Kinner.

Miss Simon's Hidden Curriculum

In an effort to understand students better, educators have recently used the tool of dividing the human into three parts or domains: the *cognitive* domain—the area of factual data and concepts built off those facts; the *affective* domain—the area of emotions, values, and feelings; and the *psychomotor* domain—the area of physical movement.

Miss Simon deals almost exclusively in the affective. She is almost the opposite of Mr. Kinner, who deals almost exclusively in the cognitive. Where he is organized; she is disorganized. He knows where he is going; she lets direction come with the moment. He puts emphasis on the written word; she emphasizes the people. He is interested in acquiring information; she is interested in watching the inner self unfold.

Miss Simon puts a high worth on the value of the human being. The individual is almost a sacred thing to her. Although she has a social classroom, the individual student is not forced into conformity. He is, on the other hand, encouraged to discover himself.

If you are one of those people who have criticized the schooling process for being a leveling monster which tries to make all the people the same, or you criticize the school for squelching the creativity out of children, then Miss Simon is your choice.

Mrs. Smith's Hidden Curriculum

Mrs. Smith is an interesting alternative to the first two. Like Mr. Kinner, she deals in the cognitive, but she does encourage socialization. The students at least will interact with her, or listen to her as she speaks to the class.

The thing that is really important in Mrs. Smith's class is Mrs. Smith—not the lesson and not the children. She has the children where they can see her. The bulletin board represents her work. She makes the decisions about what is to be learned. This is not all bad. A benevolent dictatorship may be the kindest form of government, particularly in a classroom where someone has to make some decisions.

As a traditional teacher, Mrs. Smith is interested in perpetuating the status quo. She is interested in preparing your child to live in society, not change it or fight against it. If you believe that there are certain essentials which every human being must learn in order to survive, and if you want those essentials taught to your child in a no-nonsense but caring way, Mrs. Smith is your choice.

Although it won't make much difference in the way she treats your child, it is correct that Mrs. Smith isn't as happy as she used to be. It has become rather difficult to be an enthusiastic traditionalist in today's schools. Even if you picked her first, you are not as sure about the decision as your parents would have been.

In order for Mrs. Smith to function, she must have support—support from an administration which has probably read tons of books about educational innovation and nifty teaching methods, and support from parents like yourself, who will listen to children read, turn off the television after supper, supervise arithmetic lessons, and read the notes pinned to the child's shirt when he gets home in the afternoon. Mrs. Smith is just not getting the kind of support she used to. And the other teachers probably snicker behind her back.

Mr. Huey's Hidden Curriculum

Mr. Huey doesn't like Mrs. Smith; that's for sure. Or at least, he doesn't like her teaching methods. In fact, he probably entered teaching to counteract the work of all the Mrs. Smiths in the world. He had some himself, probably learned more than he thought he did, but decided there was a better way to teach.

Like Miss Simon, Mr. Huey emphasizes the person. But where Miss Simon relies on raw native experience as a teaching vehicle, he takes the enterprise further. He wants the students to run their experiences through their rational thinking processes.

Both teachers may turn the students loose with a boa constrictor; but when the playing is over, Mr. Huey will ask some rather difficult questions. "Why did the snake skin feel bony? Why were his eyes so dim?" Those are different questions from Miss Simon's: "How did the snake feel? Did you enjoy holding it?"

Mr. Huey believes in teaching the material, but for him the material is anything that relates to the child's particular problem at that particular time. You may ask, "When *will* my child learn to divide fractions?" Mr. Huey will answer, "When he needs to." And that is his definition of learning. For him, learning goes beyond memorizing facts or studying books. Learning is applying the facts to the problem at hand. Mr. Huey won't force a child to learn anything until he has a need for it, but he will help to create a need.

Mr. Huey also emphasizes socialization. His students learn in groups. They are expected to help each other and learn from each other. This is what he calls "teaching the democratic process."

There is a kind of deceptiveness in his popularity, though. A few years ago researchers surveyed the attitudes of the seventh graders concerning school. They found that the happiest seventh graders in the nation were in classrooms more like Mrs. Smith's than Mr. Huey's. Oh, well. What does research prove?

Figuring Out Who's What

Are you still satisfied with your choice, or have you changed your mind? There isn't any penalty for being indecisive while you are reading this book, but I do hope you are prepared to make a definite decision, should you ever be confronted with the choice.

If you are still having trouble deciding which philosophy you prefer or even what difference it makes, think about the following experiences which you may encounter as a parent. Your choice of one course of action over another demonstrates your own personal philosophy of child rearing. This, in turn, should help you decide what kind of teacher your child needs.

Suppose you have a youngster at your house who is just beginning to walk. You remember the age. The child is clumsy, but inquisitive. He is constantly moving, pulling, checking, banging. By himself, he creates as much activity as a house of kittens.

How do you handle the child's development at this stage? Do you put all your good stuff away and let the child roam around at will— investigating and breaking and checking and botching? Or do you leave the good stuff out and teach that child the meaning of the word *no*?

(These are really the only two options. You may want to propose a compromise like putting away the good stuff and still teaching him to leave things alone, but that is avoiding the issue. The emphasis is still on your teaching the child to restrict his natural impulses and to get in line with social behavior. You just don't have as much confidence in your ability as a teacher as I originally purposed!)

So without compromise, which is the appropriate course of action? How you answer that question reveals a great deal about your philosophical position, and it does relate you to one of the four teachers.

For example, Miss Simon would argue that a child should never be restricted at this age. If your good stuff is that precious to you, put it away, but don't limit the child's curiosity and creativity. She would contend that letting the child get in touch with what is inside him is more important than what society demands.

Mr. Huey would probably agree with Miss Simon in part, but he would make more of the opportunity. He would try to turn the child's activities into something productive.

On the other hand, Mrs. Smith would get right to the issue. Children must learn to get along in society. They must learn that there are restrictions and limitations, that natural impulses are not always right and must be curtailed. She would leave the good things out and spank the child's grubby hands until he has learned those lessons.

Mr. Kinner would begin with the same principle as Mrs. Smith, but he would use a different technique. He would probably manufacture some kind of a reward system for when the child did leave things alone, and he would rely on his rewards more than on punishment.

For any parent, this is a real situation. Here philosophy is applied; theory becomes practice. What you do reveals your beliefs more clearly than any pronouncement you could ever make. You are an educational philosopher, whether you want to be one or not.

Let's try another test. Your son has just turned seventeen, has completed the high school driver's education course with flying colors, and has decorated his wallet with the most precious piece of paper of any American adolescent—the driver's license.

For years he has prepared for this moment. He has saved money from lawn mowing, paper routes, and part-time jobs. Now he wants wheels of his own. Cautiously you give in, and the search for the "magic pumpkin" begins. Finally, after days of diligent searching, he finds the chariot of his dreams and brings it home for your blessing before the marriage is consummated.

When he drives up, you know you are in trouble. One brief walk around the car confirms your suspicions. You see all the evidences of past abuse and imminent heartache—the worn tires, the sagging shocks, the collected crud in the exhaust pipe. But you also see the gleam in your son's eyes. And perhaps you remember some dream you once had.

What do you do? Do you exercise the prerogative of experience and forbid this purchase outright? Do you attempt to use logic and reason, knowing both will have little impact? Or do you say, "What's the use? He will learn from experience," and graciously offer your blessing?

Remember our four teachers and try to think what each would do if, as a parent, he could be true to his philosophy. Again, Mr. Huey and Miss Simon believe in the value of experience. The only way for your son to learn is to let him get involved. But Mrs. Smith and Mr. Kinner both believe that as an adult you have the obligation to prevent his suffering and financial loss.

You may never have to write the answers to questions like those, and you may never have to verbalize your thinking. But you *do* take a philosophical stand on the issues whether you want to or not. The purpose of the test is to help you identify what hidden meaning your actions have so that you can understand more clearly what a specific teacher is doing.

A Check List for Philosophy

Now that you are in touch with your own thoughts and you have some idea of what you think is best for your child, let me summarize with a check list that should help you identify the philosophical implications of a specific classroom.

Remember, we are not dealing here with good and bad. In succeeding chapters I will speak specifically about how to evaluate teachers' performances. Here, I am only interested in your being able to analyze a particular philosophical approach.

The *arrangement of furniture in a room* provides a great deal of information about the teacher. Are the desks arranged so that the students can relate to each other? Where has the teacher placed his or her desk, the symbol of authority in the classroom? Are the desks arranged in such a way as to provide ample opportunity for discussion? Is the room arrangement permanent or flexible?

Most teachers believe that *physical appearance of the classroom* is a part of the instructional process, so they work at decorating the room to reflect their teaching suppositions. You can make some rather valid assumptions about the teacher just by studying those decorations.

Is the room decorated with student-produced material or is it decorated with more professional material? If student material is used, is it material that was produced just to decorate the bulletin boards or was it assigned as a part of a larger instructional objective? Are the books in the bookcase arranged neatly? Is the teacher's desk organized or cluttered? (Although I have only observations and no statistics to prove my point, I am convinced that there is a definite correlation between neatness and noise level. Students are quieter when the books are orderly and the teacher's desk-top is visible through the papers.)

Are the bulletin boards current? Are they there for instructional purposes or decoration? Above all, if the room is decorated with student material, is the teacher proud of it? Does she call your attention to it?

Occasionally I enter a classroom as a casual visitor, knowing the venture will consume at least half an hour. Some teachers demand that every visitor see everything the students have done. I like these people. If I were in the sixth grade, I would like to be in their classes because they like children and children's ideas.

Check with your child to determine what kinds of *activities* are prominent. Usually from conversations with students you can tell how much time is allotted to discussion, direct teacher talk, individual work, films, field trips, fair projects, and other activities.

As one more measure, check to see if you can determine how dependent the teacher is on the *textbook*. Teachers who rely heavily on textbooks are usually people who believe that education is a process of cultural transmission. They have content to cover, and the book offers an efficient, organized way to get to it.

Let me emphasize again that this check list is *not* a test of quality, but a test to determine underlying presuppositions. Of course, the list is incomplete, but it should provide you with enough evidence to make a valid assumption about the philosophical position of a specific teacher.

Obviously, no teacher is going to be a pure representative of a particular position. Most teachers (like most parents) are some synthesis of all four, depending on situations and students, so don't be shocked if a "Mrs. Smith" sometimes acts like a "Mr. Huey." But I do think you can find trends which reflect presuppositions; and now that you are an educational philosopher, you are in a better position to decide what is best for your child. Once that is established, you can begin to work on the problem of teaching quality, which is the subject of Chapter 4.

Homework Assignments for Parents

1. Think back on some of your favorite teachers. What common characteristic(s) did they share? In what ways were they different?

2. How can you adjust if you think your child should have a teacher with a particular kind of approach, but gets a teacher who is just the opposite? What can you as a parent do in such a case?

3. If you were teaching, which of the described approaches would you tend to agree with most? Why?

4. As your child goes through the school system, would you prefer that he had teachers who used the same style, or an assortment of teaching approaches? Why?

4

Evaluating, Communicating, Understanding

L ike any theory, educational theory isn't much good until it is put into practice. Having a philosophy is important to the teacher, and eventually to the student, but it doesn't do much good if the teacher doesn't have the enthusiasm, compassion, and intelligence to bring it to life in the classroom.

You need to be able to distinguish between the Smiths and Kinners; but you also need to know how to distinguish between good and bad teaching. The first part of this chapter focuses on that problem. The second part offers suggestions for what to do if your child is assigned to a teacher whose incompetence overshadows his presuppositions. The third part attempts to explain why some good teachers turn sour.

Evaluating: What Makes a Teacher Good?

Teaching is a human profession and, as such, it has its flaws and weaknesses. The professional teachers don't endorse these, nor do the administrators; yet they creep in. Sometimes only the students (and their parents, if there are adequate communication channels) are aware of bad classroom procedure. Generally, students are powerless to correct these. If there is to be any improvement, the parents will have to assume responsibility. Christian parents, due to their interest in justice and skill in human relations, are desirable candidates to initiate positive action.

To simplify your task, I submit the following list of characteristics of good teachers. The list certainly reflects my bias, but it is based on years of observation. A teacher's violation of one of these points does not necessarily condemn him or her to the pedagogical junkyard, but these are points to investigate. If too many are absent, you may have a legitimate problem.

1. Good teachers read and hand back homework assignments.

Check your child's homework assignment each day and ask to look at it when it is returned. If it isn't returned, you probably should start getting concerned.

Some college students who have suspected that their fine writings were going unread have inserted into their papers such sentences as *Underline this sentence if you are still reading at this point.* They then spread the results of the investigation around campus.

I don't recommend deliberate traps, but the point is clear enough. If the work is valuable enough to justify the child's doing it, it is valuable enough to merit the teacher's reading.

2. Good teachers give worthwhile assignments.

A few years ago, I asked an intelligent high school junior to help me one evening. He replied that he couldn't because he had a long English grammar assignment. When I suggested that perhaps I could help, he said no, it was something he had to do himself. I persisted until he showed it to me.

The teacher's objective was to refresh these active, busy, high school juniors on the use of commas. The assignment was for them to copy ninety-six long sentences from a textbook and place commas in the appropriate places. Let me repeat: copy *word for word* ninety-six sentences from a text and insert commas.

I can understand teaching commas. I can even understand asking some students who are having trouble with their writing to copy sentences word for word. But this teacher was dishonest with those students. She should have typed the sentences herself and handed them to the students. This assignment grew out of a teacher's laziness.

Teachers shouldn't waste children's time on busywork. A child's time is precious. There are too many things to learn and too little time to learn them. Look at your child's homework to see whether the lessons to be learned justify the amount of time it takes him to complete the assignment.

3. Good teachers stay in the classroom.

The best way to check this is to listen to your child's stories. If he has too many tales of eraser fights and classroom chaos, the teacher may need to spend more time with the students and less at the coffee machine in the teachers' lounge.

4. Good teachers decorate their rooms.

This repeats the observations of the previous chapter, so I won't go into more detail.

5. Good teachers are organized.

Good teachers know where they are going. Students in their classes know where they are going. If your child seems to be having difficulty in determining direction or knowing what is expected of him, the teacher may not be preparing sufficiently.

Actually, poor preparation is the cause of many classroom problems. When young teachers come to me and ask for help with classroom discipline, I first ask to see their lesson plans. When a teacher has stayed up late in the night to plan an exciting and valuable lesson, he will probably demand the right to teach that lesson. Your child and every other student will profit.

6. Good teachers communicate with parents.

Teachers complain about not getting parental support, but some teachers forget to ask for it. If you discover that you are not being told about problems or that you are being told too late, you may want to investigate the teacher's energy level.

7. Good teachers don't lose control of themselves.

Interacting with twenty-five defiant youngsters is not a particularly pleasant way to spend an afternoon. Sometimes a teacher reaches his breaking point. I have full sympathy for such a person, and I understand how that can happen. But it can't be tolerated.

Teachers cannot respond to misbehavior with anger, maliciousness, or violence. The teacher must control the situation; but he has no right to ridicule, strike in anger, or abuse a student. There is no room in the profession for teachers who react this way.

8. Good teachers don't lose control of the classroom.

For the last ten years the Gallup Poll, as published each fall in the *Phi Delta Kappan* magazine, has indicated that lack of discipline is considered the number one problem in American schools. Lack of discipline is a problem. Rowdiness and destruction are rampant. Schools have initiated a plethora of sociologically and psychologically sound programs in an attempt to restore order. But programs fail when there are no people to carry them out.

There is no single technique or sure-fire method for establishing control, but good teachers will do whatever it takes to remain in charge. Of course, not all silent classes are in control, and not all noisy ones are out of control. A teacher is in control when the students are responding to his direction and objectives for the class.

9. Good teachers give students a sense that the material is important.

Educators talk about motivation, though most of us don't even know what the animal looks like. But if your child rushes home with a burning desire to do homework just as Mrs. Doe suggested, Mrs. Doe is probably a good teacher.

10. Good teachers don't abuse their right to academic freedom.

Each year I go to one of the local high schools and lecture to the seniors. The purpose is purely methodological. The teacher wants to train the students in listening and taking notes, skills which are vital to college success.

Since the objective is method instead of content, I get to pick the topic. I once talked about the history of first-century Rome—a thrilling subject, relevant to dynamic seventeen year olds. I warned them at the beginning that I was going to interject personal opinion and half-truth into the data, and challenged them to sort through this and demand proof.

After talking loud and fast for about forty-five minutes, I gave a short quiz. One of the questions was, "True or False: Rome fell because it did not have a valid program of planned obsolescence."

That question is as loaded as a missile silo. It is a question of economic theory presented as a question of economic fact. No matter how he responds, the student has endorsed an opinion, and his "objective" grade will be based on the opinion he endorses.

This question is illegal. This procedure is illegal. Teachers *cannot* teach this way.

I am a strong supporter of academic freedom, particularly when I can define what it is; but a teacher does not have a right to offend a child. By law, teachers can't teach religion in public schools. By the same law, they can't ridicule it, either. We need to realize that some Supreme Court cases *protect* Christians as well as limit them. Teachers cannot use the classroom for a showcase of personal beliefs, values, or life-styles.

As a member of the human race, a teacher has every right to be what he is. But he cannot use his position of authority to persuade, and he cannot present opinion as fact.

Communicating: How to Get Results

Just reading the above list isn't going to make you an expert on teacher evaluation. Educational scientists themselves have difficulty agreeing on the difference between good and bad teaching. But you should at least have some idea as to what your child's comments reveal about his teacher. I wouldn't be too alarmed by stories of isolated incidents similar to some in the above list, but if you begin to detect a frequency or a trend, you may need to exercise your right as a taxpayer and concerned parent.

When that time comes, however, it is important for you to do it right. If you make the wrong moves here, not only could you be ineffective, you might be damaging. So I offer the following list of rules, tempered from a teacher's point of view. I want you to be heard; I want the situation to be corrected; but I think I understand how to speak to teachers in a way that gets the best results.

1. Don't yell "Wolf!"

If you shout too much about every little thing, you will soon develop laryngitis and no one will hear you. Reserve your school visits for significant injustices. If you are fortunate, you may never have to go—at least, not for the purpose of confrontation.

2. Get all the facts.

I would never imply that your child might lie, but some do. Sometimes children get so involved in telling a story that they lose sight of the boundary between fact and fiction. And perceptions themselves are sometimes distorted in the heat of the moment.

The big boys might not have really set fire to the paper in the bathroom. The teacher may not be as rude as he seems to a fourth grader. These do make interesting stories, and everything your child tells you merits your attention, but just make sure you have both sides of the situation.

3. Try to understand the problem from the teacher's point of view.

A few years ago, I met a teacher who had been highly recommended by both his former and present students. Yet I found him negative, abrupt, and abrasive. I decided the students had overrated him. Later, I learned that his wife had died about a month before our first meeting. The students knew this, and they were willing to allow him time to mourn his loss.

Always remember that there may be extenuating circumstances that must be considered.

4. Go straight to the source.

If the teacher is inadequate, he is the one to whom you need to address the problem. Go to him first. If he doesn't respond, go through the appropriate chain of command. But start with the teacher.

5. Don't put the teacher on the defensive.

Don't go if you are angry. Wait until you cool down and the two of you can discuss the situation calmly.

6. Don't be afraid to compliment a teacher.

You are then in a better position to take issue with him later. A brief note of appreciation for some specific lesson or act can go a long way in making a teacher happier with his salary, and paper isn't all that expensive. Besides, he will get the idea that you have good judgment.

7. Don't make the teacher feel worse than he already does.

If you go visit a teacher for something he has done in a fit of passion, don't be surprised to find him already remorseful. In that case, he needs your friendship, not your sharp tongue. Good teachers sometimes make mistakes, but they are aware of them. They don't need you to point them out.

8. Always approach a teacher with the purpose of correcting the problem.

If the situation gets so bad that you feel you have to make your appearance, don't go with the idea that you are going to get someone fired. Part of the Gospel, the good news of our Savior, is that people can change. As a Christian, your only purpose can be to hope to correct the situation, to make things better for the children in the classroom. And it might not hurt for you to believe in the teacher's ability to improve.

9. Remember individual differences.

The first step in your becoming an educational asset to your child is to become objective about his uniqueness. If you need help understanding this, visit the teacher. He probably has analyzed the situation.

Because of the nature of classrooms, teachers must teach to the norm, the average. If your child doesn't fit into that norm, then that is your problem. He will need your patience and your supplementary help. Don't label a teacher as bad simply because he is not reaching one child.

Don't forget that there are children at both ends of the norm. Your child may need special attention in a specific skill because he has a different learning style. Your child may also need special attention because he learns faster than the normal child. Frequently, the results are similar for both extremes.

Good teachers know these things and see them developing. But unfortunately, when a teacher has thirty unique human creations in a classroom, he simply can't anticipate and correct every tendency.

10. Don't sue.

Look! I'm a taxpayer, too. To sue the public school is to sue yourself. If you have a point to prove, there are cheaper ways to go about it. Check to see how much legal fees have increased in your district's budget during the past five years.

Understanding: Why Good Teachers Wear Out

Every year I teach scores of college seniors who plan to enter the field. Every one of those bright, eager, young people intends to be good. I doubt that there is a weak teacher anywhere who once said during his college days, "I think I'll be a teacher, and I think I will be bad at it."

Sometimes young teachers are not as good as they should be, because they lack experience and adequate preparation. If they survive the first few years without permanently damaging young lives and the American society, they could become good teachers.

On the other hand, teachers frequently start out with a burst of enthusiasm, creativity, and effectiveness, and through the years deteriorate into weak, bland, disinterested teachers. These people don't seem to improve with experience. They just continue to stay in the classroom, the Exhibit C's of the first chapter, and dream of retirement in some village which is off limits to anyone below twenty-one.

Those teachers who lose their enthusiasm and effectiveness over a period of years present a major problem to the quality of American education. I don't have some magic solution for reversing the trend, nor do I have much advice for helping renew any specific teacher; but I would like to offer some reasons for this problem occurring. Again, these reasons are from a teacher's point of view, but that view may help you understand some of the pressures which will eventually affect your child's education.

1. Teaching is a continuous-pressure job.

I hear those comments about the long vacations and short days, but teaching is still a pressure activity. A shoe salesman may stay at the store a little longer than a teacher stays at school, but when the salesman goes home at night, he probably realizes he is finished for the day. There is nothing he can do during that time at home to make himself a more effective shoe salesman.

A teacher, on the other hand, especially a good teacher, has very few evenings in his life when he is free from the tyranny of tomorrow's lesson. Regardless of how prepared he may be, he can always prepare some more. There is always another book on the subject which he has never read. There is always a school activity where his students are demonstrating their talents. There are papers to be read, records to keep, plans to be made. For a good teacher the day never ends; he just decides he must quit. In the past twenty years, I have never gone to bed feeling that I have finished for the day.

Some teachers may not always respond to the pressure, but just knowing it is there will eventually make one weary.

2. Good teaching doesn't have many immediate results.

Regardless of what surface reasons teachers use for getting into the profession, most of us had, somewhere in the bottoms of our minds, some idea that we were going to make the world better. And we may be doing that, but it will be at least twenty years before we know. In the meantime, we busy ourselves with earthshaking issues such as the difference between a B and a C grade, gum chewing versus no gum chewing, and the five reasons for the French Revolution.

While teachers are doing this year after year, parents watch their children grow through the impetuousness of childhood, the awkwardness of early adolescence, the seriousness of later adolescence, the experimentation of early adulthood, and the fulfillment of life. If your child makes it through all these stages and turns out all right, you are going to rejoice in it—but that fourth-grade teacher will still be collecting milk money and settling playground squabbles.

3. Teachers don't get paid much.

I am not trying to solicit sympathy, but this is a fact of life. Teachers' salaries are actually relative, according to the local standard of living. In some places salaries are sufficient to permit the teacher to enjoy a standard of living equal to most of the other people in the community. If this is so, teachers don't really deserve sympathy.

But in many affluent communities, salaries will not permit teachers the same standard of living. I don't feel sorry for the teacher; he knew what the salary scale was when he entered the profession. But this lower standard of living also means that the teacher's family must sacrifice because the wage earner chose that profession. At this point in his life, a teacher-parent may get grumpy when he must continuously tell his own children that they can't keep up with the kids down the block.

4. Teaching is an extension of one's personality.

I am sure most people have a sense of pride about their work. None of us likes to be told that we are not good at what we do. But because teaching requires so much ego involvement, teachers are very vulnerable to criticism.

I have known some rather competent teachers who have been almost destroyed by critical remarks made by their superiors, their students, or parents of their students. Listening to those kinds of remarks too long will make even the strong become defensive, paranoid, or apathetic.

Teaching is something that involves my personality, my very personhood. If you tell me that I am not a good teacher, you have not merely assessed a skill, you have attacked me as a person.

I have not offered the above list to solicit your sympathy. Nor do I propose that you rush out and start some charitable cause for old, worn-out teachers. I simply want to introduce you to the pressures which thoughtful, caring, giving teachers face.

Of course, everyone faces pressures in his work, and there are certainly pressures in being a parent. But if, in your mission to help your child survive and thrive, you ever have to confront bad teaching, you need to have some understanding of those pressures unique to teachers. Without that understanding, there will be no effective communication, and without effective communication there will be no positive change.

I also intend for the above list to lead us to a reassuring conclusion to this sometimes negative chapter. Teachers are human. As such they have weaknesses and they make mistakes. Parents who are interested in their child's education must be alert to the possibility of incompetence and error. But most teachers are actually rather nice people.

Your child's teacher may not be getting the job done. He may be making some noticeable mistakes. But despite all that, he is probably a pretty decent sort. In all my associations with teachers in five states, I have only met a few who were vicious or mean or petty by basic nature, and those people didn't stay in the profession too long.

If you can remember this, you will be more effective as an educational evaluator, you will be more effective as an agent of pedagogical improvement, and you will be more effective as a parent whose primary motivation is to do what is best for your child.

Homework Assignments for Parents

1. Have you ever confronted a teacher whom you thought wasn't doing an adequate job? After reading this chapter, would you have handled the situation the same way?

2. Is your relationship with your child open enough for you to be able to evaluate his teacher's performance? Or do you need to do a little more prodding to motivate your child to talk more about his school and teacher?

3. What things could you begin to do to take some of the pressure and monotony out of your child's teacher's job? What could the teacher do to keep you better informed? Meet together and discuss your ideas.

5

Two Tough Issues for the School

I n Chapters 2—4, I have concentrated on the individual classroom teacher. For a given child, this is the appropriate focus. Good teachers can turn almost any program into great educational experiences. Weak teachers will always yield unsatisfactory results regardless of the quality of the program.

However, in this concluding chapter, I want to broaden the perspective by including a discussion of the school system itself. Here I would like to focus on some of the problems which are currently perplexing educators, complicating the purpose of schools, and affecting educational quality.

You could entertain yourself on a rainy Saturday afternoon developing a long list enumerating all these problems, but it wouldn't be all that profitable. So rather than list a multitude of problems, I will discuss only two—the school's role as a social healer, and the deteriorating family.

The School as Social Healer

In contemporary American society, schools have been given the primary responsibility for doctoring every social disease we encounter. When people began to wreck their lives in automobile accidents, the schools proposed to correct the situation with driver's education. When middle-aged America became fat, flabby, and susceptible to early heart attacks, state lawmakers solved the problem by making physical education compulsory for children. When young people were seduced into free love, venereal disease, and unwanted pregnancies, the schools implemented a program of correction with another ambiguous pill called sex education. When drug abuse duped our adolescents and young adults, the schools were mandated by law to correct the problem with something in the curriculum called drug education.

And the beat goes on. Some of the offerings around the nation include courses in such things as death and dying, values, responsibility, consumer knowledge, capitalism, race problems, and hygiene. This is what some educators call the "add-a-course mentality." It makes no difference what the problem is or how elusive its solution, the school can just add a course as an instant cure. But answers don't come as easily as it may seem.

Quite frequently, professional educators have had the responsibility of correction mandated to them by law, not by choice. They don't know how to accomplish it. The idea that anything can be made into a course of study is wrong.

Educators know that a course contains goals, a body of knowledge, text materials, and some kind of objective evaluation system. So a course in sex differs from a course in history only in content. The procedure is the same: the student learns the material, takes a test, gets a grade in the grade book, and lives happily ever after. But this is not what the lawmakers had in mind when they mandated the course.

A very subtle trap lies here. Unfortunately, some very fine educators, even some Christian educators, have been snared. Creative thought has been invested in designing efficient and ethical techniques for schools to teach values, but that is not the issue.

At issue is the educational costs of such programs, regardless of how effective they might be. The issue is still concentrated on reading scores, composition skills, and standardized test scores. It is naive to assume that the schools are equipped to cure social ills when they haven't even mastered their original purpose—cognitive and intellectual development.

All this responsibility for social doctoring presents a rather interesting paradox. It comes at a time when pollsters tell us that the public has lost confidence in the schools to fulfill their roles. Yet lawmakers and the public alike are still thrusting schools into added and more difficult tasks. The schools are in a no-win situation, and most school people are aware of this. They need help. There is still a big gap between football offenses and haircuts.

The Deteriorating Family

One spring day, I was standing in the hall of a junior high school when a student came merrily along, whistling a happy tune. A teacher stopped him and said, "We missed you in class yesterday."

The young man thought for a moment, and then reported his absence. "Oh, yeah. I forgot to tell you. My real dad died out in Iowa, and we had to go to the funeral." With that he continued whistling his way down the hall.

The nuclear family may not be a dead institution, but it is definitely not the picture of health. The statistics are provocative. Nearly one-half of all marriage contracts are now broken before they reach maturity. More than forty percent of all children enrolled in school come from a home of fewer than two parents. These are national averages. In some neighborhoods and communities the percentages are even greater.

But cold statistics are based on living realities. In fact, we have heard those statistics so often that we run the risk of becoming insensitive to their meaning. Behind each statistic is a human being who deserves our sensitivity. The father-child relationship is so sacred that it serves as the metaphor of a person's relationship to his Creator.

Yet, I have known children who have had as many as four different fathers before they reached junior high school. How many times can we rip such a sacred commitment from a child's life and expect him to keep his stability? I am simply not prepared to teach in a world where young adolescents are so emotionally confused that they cannot grieve the death of their own fathers.

This is more disturbing than it sounds. For two centuries, the American schools have worked hand in hand with the family in rearing children. They were, for the most part, mutually supportive agencies. Children knew about this relationship, and they knew they could depend on it.

Several of us had this confirmed when we were told, "If you get spanked at school, you can expect the same when you get home." We may have suspected a conspiracy, but we realized the unity of authority, the cooperation between home and school. Now in many homes, the parents say, "If you get spanked in school, we will call the lawyer when you get home."

For two centuries the schools have depended on the family to teach children some important lessons about life—response to authority, the desire to learn, the value of honesty, the meaning of respect, the purpose of punctuality. Now there is no family, at least not a dependable one, to teach those lessons.

Schools are caught in the middle. Without the family teaching its designated lessons, educational systems aren't as effective as they should be. The normal reaction would be for the school to try to correct the problem or at least try to compensate. They have attempted to do this in two ways.

Schools, in many instances, have tried to become a substitute family—to fill the gaps created when the family doesn't exist or isn't functioning as an educational agent. Many administrators aim their extracurricular programs at these gaps. They reason, "If the child can't go home, at least he can go to the gym for basketball practice."

The other way in which schools have attempted to correct the problem of the missing family is to teach young people the importance of family relationships and values. Schools often offer complete courses in such things as home, values, family relations, and family living. Some of these courses appear to be innovative and exciting, at least on paper.

But they all suffer one possible pedagogical weakness: In order for young people to learn these lessons, they must have role models, they must come from homes—or at least know about homes—where the textbook values are being applied. Many young people don't have access to such models, so in these cases, schools seem to be teaching impractical ideals.

Both these attempts by the schools—to become a substitute family and to teach family values—have met an avalanche of criticism, some from guerrilla fighters and some from organized movements. The opponents protest that schools aren't designed to teach these kinds of lessons, that the original purpose of schools is being weakened, that the homes should teach the values and the merits of successful family living.

Most educators agree, but they have been forced into their roles. This is the paradox. Society has placed demands on schools that the schools can't meet. Yet, when the educators do attempt to meet those demands, they are criticized for their efforts. A search for a solution to this dilemma brings us back to the underlying thesis of this book. Your child is going to have a better chance of surviving and perhaps even thriving in the world of adolescence if he can get a sense that the school and the home are working together toward a common end.

By this time, I hope that you are becoming familiar with that mysterious monster called the school. I hope that you are familiar enough with the school and with the general attitudes of teachers that you are at least not afraid of them anymore. I hope you are familiar enough to begin to believe that most school people really do have good intentions despite how it may seem to an outsider. I hope that you are familiar enough with schools to be an agent of positive correction should there be something which needs correcting.

Now that you know something about the schools, it is time for you to begin to understand another major force in your child's education: parents.

Homework Assignments for Parents

1. What socially oriented programs are available in your child's school? How do you feel about each of them? Have you expressed your opinions to the school?

2. Where do you feel that the school is inadequate to sufficiently train your child (sex education, driver's education, or whatever)? What are you doing to address your child's needs instead? What more do you need to be doing?

3. As a parent, what kind of social models are you providing for your child? If you are a single parent, what can you do to help your child receive some needed role modeling by an adult of the other sex?

4. Can you identify any areas of your child's life over which you have been giving the school total control? If so, what do you need to do to ensure that your child knows that you are still the authority over such activities?

SECTION 2:
THE POWER OF
THE FAMILY

6

The Nucleus
of the Family

In every small town I have ever known there is something I call the "town family." Although each town family is distinctive, there are some general traits. First, there are too many children; usually, this is the largest family in town. Their house is the most unattractive in the community—old, in need of repairs and paint, ill-kept. Generally, the family has some really despicable habit which contributes to the blight. They keep chickens or rabbits or have a huge population of dogs and cats to match the children. There is never any grass in the lawn; it is worn bare by traffic. Old, abandoned cars are the only decorative items.

The children live with independence and mobility. They have no first names when they get away from the house; the community knows each as "one of those Smith kids." Teachers sometimes don't even call them by first names. The children pick up odd jobs, hunt for pop cans along the road, and accept handouts.

Father's salary is never adequate, so the community begrudges them luxuries. If the family gets a new possession, such as a TV, the community gossips, "What do they need with a TV? Why don't they spend that money on food and clothes for all those kids?" Yet, the parents take vacations and weekends away, leaving the children at home to fend for themselves and contributing further material for the gossip mills.

However, when we successful people meet back in that town for ten-year reunions, we are always surprised. One of those children is now a doctor; another is a lawyer; another is a scientist. At the frequent family get-togethers, the whole block is covered with big cars and happy people. Sometimes we can gossip about this all evening.

Since I have seen this happen so often—children rising out of obscurity and deprivation to meet life and conquer it—I have tried to look for a pattern, a hint. What was it that indicated that these young people were going to grow into healthy, intelligent, success-oriented adults? In retrospect, I think I have discovered something. In every case, these children demonstrated a deep and abiding loyalty to family.

While the rest of the community was telling me what a desperate scoundrel the father was, the children were quoting him in class as if he were the ultimate authority on matters. Mother worked, but she also darned the socks, washed the necks, and refereed when she thought someone was taking advantage of one of her children. In school corridors, older brothers and sisters would stop and tease the younger ones, even when they were avoided by most of the other children.

At one time in my life, I thought those parents had so many children because they were ignorant. Now I've decided they had so many children because they had a great capacity to love.

As a parent, I have worried about what gifts I can give my children. An education? An appreciation of the value of hard work? Straight teeth? A knowledge of God? A color television? An automobile at sixteen? But in the light of what I have learned from all the "town families" I have ever known, I wonder whether I can give them a feeling for the spirit of family. I want to, and it is from this desire that I write this section.

The Family Heartbeat

For the Christian, the first (and possibly ultimate) line of defense against the problems and inadequacies of the public school is the family. This statement is not really a contradiction to the preceding chapter about the declining family.

It is true that the nuclear family is a very feeble institution in contemporary society, and it is probably also true that it is not about to encounter some miraculous and instantaneous recovery. But for parents who are concerned about the quality of life for their children and the quality of their preparation for adulthood, strengthening the family remains the number one priority.

Throughout this book I make suggestions about how a Christian can have some input into what is happening in the schools; but all this input still doesn't guarantee that the child is going to be well-educated. Despite the specialized nature of human services, *the parents are still the primary educators*—not the teachers and not the schools.

By definition, the *nuclear family* has a "nucleus"—a center, a heart, a hub, a vibrant and dynamic organ around which the family moves and finds its identity. A philosopher suggested that community results when the members relate to a *common other.* If the family is a community (or a unit of people who communicate), it must have a definite common other to which all members relate.

I am willing to take this idea further and maintain that all members of the community must be an equal distance from the common other. In other words, if I place some common other first in my life, but my wife places it third and my children place it fifth or even lower, we won't have much of a community or family life. We must relate to the common point from equal distances; and, preferably, it should be the number one priority for each of us.

Historically, throughout the Western world, the nucleus of the family has not been so elusive as it has become in recent years. I was reared on a farm (and in an earlier generation). Every member of the family knew what was the center of life, and we all related to it equally. We knew what ultimately made all decisions. Those decisions might have been interpreted by our mother or father, but the farm decided what time we would get up, when we would go on vacation, whether we could buy something, whether we could participate in extracurricular activities. Since the farm had almost complete power over our lives, we gave it a large amount of our devotion. It was first in our minds as well as first in our lives.

What, then, is the nucleus of your family? What is the heart around which all members move? Is it a house? Probably not, if you are in an average family. The house is viewed as an investment or a stepping-stone into a nicer house.

Is it the father's job? Perhaps so in your house. But I have talked with children whose fathers are high-ranking executives in some of the most powerful firms in the nation. When I ask them what their fathers do, they report, "He works in the Loop." Translated, that means he gets on a commuter train every morning and disappears into existential nothingness until seven o'clock that evening. These men may be controlling the destiny of the nation, but their own children have no concept of the nature of their work or its importance.

The next logical question is whether the nucleus has to be a tangible thing. I would *like* to answer with a resounding no. It would be nice to think that people could be united around a noble theme such as love, commitment to God, or even ethical integrity. But I am not convinced they can.

I have heard pastors proclaim that the only way to keep a congregation working together is to keep it in debt. That is a rather strong commentary on our confidence in the power of God moving throughout the membership. But most communities and pseudocommunities to which I belong manufacture artificial tangibles to promote harmony and cooperation.

Some family prophets have proposed this same kind of artificial nucleus building, and some families have used the advice with good results. For example, family counselors suggest that we reserve one night a week for "family night." In certain families this special night has become quite successful. All members work hard to stay free of other commitments for that night, and the family plans as a unit and plays as a unit. This may sound like a token attempt, but if Thursday night is the only thing a family has in common, thank God for Thursday night. At least, these people have some kind of a nucleus.

In my profession, I encounter families in which a central cause is an activity of one of the children. Sports commonly serve this function. If one of the sons is a football player, the family finds some harmony in that football career. Family members wait for meals until practice is over, travel together to the games, and generally plan their lives around the schedule. Again, this may sound like a token effort, but if families find unity in this, thank God for football.

I am not trying to be a prophet of doom, but there are two obvious points we all must accept:

1. *The nucleus of your family, if your family is a fairly typical suburban or urban household, is not a natural consequence of your coming together and living together. It must be determined and specified.*

2. *There are more things in your environment to splinter your family than to bring it together.*

What's Fighting the Family?

Some of these splinter agents are obvious, but most are quite discreet. You pledge a measure of loyalty to them quite innocently; but before you realize it, they have split your family into a thousand directions.

Clubs and organizations, despite their worth, have this effect. Who among us has not had the experience of planning a rather exciting family outing before we realize that it's the night for the Girl Scout meeting?

Some *churches* are excellent splinter agents. One child goes to Awana on Monday. Mother attends the ladies' group meeting on Tuesday. The whole family may go to prayer meeting on Wednesday, but children have their own session. Father works in visitation on Thursday. Another child goes to a youth meeting on Friday. The parents attend an adult picnic on Saturday. On Sunday, they all go to church, of course, but the young people sit in a specified section, rows away from the parents; and they all listen to the preacher deliver an inspiring sermon about the need for a strong family.

Frequently, our own *opulence* is a splintering agent. In this generation, most American families are using more space than at any other time in history. Recently, I was visiting a young couple with two small children. They were planning an addition to their house because they just did not have enough space. I agreed and was feeling sorry for them, until I realized that the parents who built the house had reared six children there.

Central heat is a splinter agent. When we lived in that old, breezy farmhouse that was heated with one small coal stove, the family met on regular occasions. As soon as we got up, every time we came into the house, and right before we went to bed, we had family meetings—right in front of the stove. Our meetings weren't called or planned, but they were functional. With central heat, members of the family can disappear and not surface for days.

I suspect our generation, those of us who are now parents of adolescents and children, grew up watching too much "Leave It to Beaver" on television. Somewhere I got the idea that a good family is one that provides a room for each child. In good families each child goes to his room to study, to play, to contemplate, or to wait for dinner. For years, I tried to run my family with this mistaken notion. After all these years of fighting children, I have finally interpreted what they are trying to tell me.

Good families have a family shrine, an altar, a central meeting place. And in good families, children like to spend most of their time at that shrine. The shrine may be the television set, the living room, the dining room table, or perhaps even the parents' bedroom; but it is the central meeting place, the replacement of the old, coal stove. It represents the family, and the children go there when they need support or just want to feel warm.

Although my mother doesn't have children at home anymore, she has learned this lesson from her dog. She pours the dog food into his dish in the kitchen. However, throughout the day and evening, the dog will run into the kitchen with a sudden urge, grab a huge mouthful of dog biscuits, rush back to the living room (where my mother spends most of the day), spit the excess biscuits on the carpet, and then proceed to eat his meals at the family shrine. He knows the meaning of togetherness.

Resisting the Splintering Agents

All this can be summarized in a few simple sentences. If your family is going to work, you have to *make* it work. It won't work by accident. If your family doesn't work, all the other energies you spend trying to control and direct your children's education will be so much wasted effort.

Begin today. Identify your nucleus. If you don't have one, build one. To that end, let me offer a few suggestions. None of these come with any kind of guarantee. They are only things I have observed other families use with success.

1. Develop a daily ritual of family devotions.

I know this is the same sermon the preacher has been yelling for years, but in this age of space and splinters, it is not bad advice for family development as well as spiritual growth. You don't have to be a master teacher or a theologian. Just meet and read some Scripture. If you can't read, play a tape. The meeting is as important as the message.

2. Eat at least one meal a day together.

Recently, I asked a group of college seniors to identify their most memorable childhood experience. One stable young man who is a member of a large, working family answered, "Breakfasts." He explained that the family met at breakfast each morning to discuss the day, catch up on the news, share, and eat. To him, it was more than a meal; it was a relationship. I know this isn't always easy to do, but making a family work is never easy. You have to start somewhere and pray for God's blessing.

3. Develop a family hobby.

Be careful not to force this, but if the parents and children can find something they all like to do, the hobby can become a great nucleus. I know one family where each member jogs. As crazy and clannish as joggers are by nature, this makes the ideal hobby. They come together in their reading materials, their pains, their joys, and their races. In addition, they are all in good health.

Other hobbies that can accomplish family unity are such things as rock collecting, model building, doing needlepoint, and painting. The beginning of the hobby can come from two directions. It can be parent-initiated or child-initiated. If you don't have a family hobby, you might begin by studying some of your child's interests. You may find something broad enough to get the whole family involved.

4. Get a family pet.

Animals frequently provide good therapy, and they can unite just because of the demands of care. Pets are good instruments for teaching such family lessons as unselfishness. When the necessity of the dog's trip outside coincides with a favorite television program, someone has to experience the sacrifice of love. Some psychologists are recommending pet therapy for emotionally disturbed children.

One parent whose children satisfactorily endured maturation during the difficult late sixties told me that he attributed all the success to the family horse which demanded much attention that would have otherwise been misdirected. Besides, pets serve as excellent workbooks for the lessons in sex education which most parents dread.

5. Take a family vacation.

Again, be careful about forcing children to do something they may not enjoy, but a well-planned vacation might be the highlight of your child's youth. If you can't afford such a vacation, borrow the money. Financial problems will always be with us, but our children soon grow up and leave. Camping families rank high among the happiest families I know.

6. Share your work with your children.

I have heard those protests that we should leave our work at the office if we want to ensure mental and social health. But parents who are happy with their work will want to share it. They want their children to know the pleasure of being productive. If they invite the children to help with some of the tasks, the children can feel that they are part of the economic scene as well. If parents are not happy in their work, that is another kind of problem.

Identifying Your Nucleus: A Family Test

In our family, my profession is the nucleus. Regardless of how chauvinistic that may sound, it is a reality. My wife and children know where and what I teach. They know my students. They know my strengths and weaknesses. They help open our home to students. They help me prepare materials. They visit my office and classroom. They plan activities around my teaching schedule. Thus, they have no quarrels about spending my money or basking in whatever glory might come as a result of my career. We are a family.

If you are still having trouble determining the nucleus of your family, let me offer one additional suggestion, a family exam. Call your brood together and get them into a less-than-hostile mood.

You may want to feed them ice cream and cake, tell them you have just bought a new car, or whatever it takes to make the group cheerful. When you get the proper atmosphere, suggest a family game. You may distribute paper and pencil and let them write their answers, or you may want to rely on the old family-circle discussion device. The method depends on the members' ability to share their feelings with each other.

Now I suggest the following activities. You may not want to use all the examples, but the first rule of teaching is to be overprepared, so at least have the whole list available.

1. Tell us what you would miss most if you were held hostage for 444 days and couldn't come back to this house.

Make sure you point out that the family member is only held hostage from the home. Don't deny him his right to Americana such as hot dogs and discount stores.

Study the answers you get to this question. You may see a trend. Will they miss other family members and relationships, or things and events?

I am not going to make any generalizations about what those answers mean. I would have to know more about your specific family. But you should be able to tell what things are perceived as most important to your family members.

2. Recall a previous year and something significant about it.

How far back you go depends on how old your children are. Don't go back beyond anyone's memory. Again, consider the answers. See what is remembered and note what will be left when the present passes into the past.

What a person remembers tells us a lot about what is important to him. Incidentally, now that my siblings and I have all become senile and grumpy, we play this game by the hours. It is fun to see how our perceptions of a given event compare.

3. Remember a moment or event when someone in the family embarrassed you.

The answers to this question will tell you what the member values personally.

4. Remember a moment or event when some family member made you happy to be part of this family.

This will give you the same kind of information as number 3, but in a more positive way.

5. Make a list of dos and don'ts of child rearing.

Make sure your children participate. Tell them to think about what they are going to do when they have their own families. I suggest this only if you have the courage to hear the truth. Children can be quite candid.

In "The Death of the Hired Man," Robert Frost wrote, "Home is the place where, when you have to go there, they have to take you in." What is it about your home which makes the family members come home when they can't go anywhere else? This is your nucleus.

Homework Assignments for Parents

1. What is the nucleus of your family? Give your own answer, and then test other family members to see if they come up with the same thing.

2. By now, you're probably familiar with your child's school activities. But how much do your children know about what you and your spouse do? What are some ways you can creatively inform them about your career(s)?

3. If your family is becoming splintered, what are some things you can do to bring everyone together once in a while? Be specific in planning, and then be sure to put your plan into action.

7

Lessons Only Home Can Teach

For years, serious demonstrations of disruptive behavior have resulted in students being suspended. School officials reasoned that at the point of the infraction the student needed a firmer reprimand than the school was equipped to issue, and that the student needed some lesson in basic human behavior which the school was not equipped to teach. So they sent the child home for a specified number of days. Supposedly, the student came back to school humble, contrite, appreciative, and schooled in the art of graceful living.

Now, we have something called "in-school suspension." The original principle is still there—a student guilty of serious disruptive behavior must be separated from his peers and from the mainstream of school activity until he becomes humble, contrite, appreciative, and schooled in the art of graceful living. But now we don't send him home. We keep him at school in a room designated for students on suspension.

The students come each morning and report to the room where they spend the day, suspended from class and other school activities. Teachers are assigned to supervise that room. I suspect that principals in charge of in-school suspension search their faculties for the most ill-mannered folk, but teachers tell me that their assignment to supervision duty is a cruel and unusual punishment. Nevertheless, the students are forced to sit in the room without the privileges of socializing with their colleagues or participating in classroom activities. When they have served their specified number of days, they return to their normal routine.

Why did school people see a need to shift the location of the suspension from the home back to the school? When officials suspended students from school and sent them back to their parents, they really believed that the parents were going to teach the students something important about cooperative living. Evidently school officials don't believe that anymore. It is apparent that school people still want students to learn something about socially acceptable behavior while they are being punished. And it is also apparent that the educators feel those lessons are now better taught in school rather than at home.

This reasoning bothers me. For centuries, school people have depended on the home to teach the students certain integral lessons. When those lessons were taught at home, the school could more effectively teach what it was designed to teach. In spite of all we may know about social relationships, learning theory, educational methodology, human values, and behavior modification, not all that much has changed.

Basically the schools are doing what they are capable of doing. But there are some lessons, some very important lessons, which they cannot teach well. Four of these, which we will examine more closely in this chapter, are *self-worth, a sense of belonging, respect for authority, and a desire to learn.*

If your child is going to learn these lessons, he needs to learn them from you. And if he learns these lessons from you, he will be in a better position to learn the lessons the schools can and do teach.

Self-Worth

Any teacher who is worth his salt or his salary will admit that he can't teach a child much unless the child has a good image of himself. Some children come to school with a positive self-image—confident that they can master history, literature, or science; but many others don't have such an image. Good teachers then make an attempt to build it, but what teachers build is usually self-esteem rather than self-worth.

Self-worth results when a person is satisfied with his own existence and does not need to make apologies for being. *Self-esteem* comes from comparing oneself with someone else and coming out on top. For the gifted, it is easy. The student who has medals and patches hanging from his athletic jacket has little trouble with a self-image. A shy or less aggressive child has more difficulty.

Teachers attack low self-images with competitive situations designed to let the child succeed. Thus, the result is self-esteem. "Sarah won the spelling bee today." "Joe is the best baseball player in the class." "Johnny is the best chalkboard eraser I have ever had." This is actually good teaching. It is quick, and it gets good results.

Students who feel good about themselves, either from self-worth or self-esteem, perform better. They are happier, more pleasant, more industrious. But even the best teacher cannot possibly reach every student with an image-building situation. If your child is going to learn the lesson of self-worth, you are going to have to teach it to him.

This isn't easy. Again, opulence is an enemy. The best teacher of self-worth is human productivity—justifying one's existence by contributing something to the world. In previous generations, this was an easier thing to provide for children.

As a member of a farm family, I became a part of the economic force about as soon as I became aware of my own existence. Because I was alive, we were able to milk more cows, plant more cotton, grow more potatoes. I knew I was an important human being because I was producing.

On the other hand, your children have been financial liabilities all their lives, and you need to be careful not to communicate that fact to them. They suspect it, and any little hint makes them feel guilty and destroys their feelings of self-worth.

This has become increasingly apparent as we continue to postpone adulthood. Physiologically, a person is an adult at thirteen or fourteen years old. This is a biological certainty. Mary was probably that age when she gave birth to our Savior. But culture has changed that.

Presently, culture is postponing adulthood as long as possible—hoping to keep people from uniting in marriage, reproducing, or joining the labor force. For some, "adolescence" goes on into the mid-twenties. How far can we stretch the gap between biological maturity and cultural maturity and still maintain a sane society of young adults?

How are you relating to your children so that they know they are not economic liabilities or cultural castoffs eternally trapped in a holding pattern? What are you doing to promote their sense of self-worth? I have a few suggestions. Add others of your own.

1. Acknowledge your child's existence occasionally.

Just take time to stop and say, "You sure bring me a lot of joy. I am really happy you are my child." This is probably most profitable when it comes at an unexpected time. It isn't hard to do if your child has, for some reason, just kissed you on the cheek or has just shown you a straight-A report card. But the statement is much more effective after he has just dropped and broken your hard-earned bowling trophy or spilled ink on the new carpet.

2. Give the child responsibility.

Children are interesting creatures. They may protest their chores in loud tones, but they find distinction in them. Don't be afraid to trust your children with serious and adultlike responsibilities, and you may not need much more. I heard one person proclaim that bottled milk is the curse of contemporary child rearing. If every family had to keep its own cow, children would be happier and better students. If you don't have a cow, create the equivalent of one.

3. Use praise judiciously.

If your child deserves good words for something he has done, praise him promptly and sincerely. But don't brag about him for insignificant or shoddy production. He knows the difference, and he will see through your game quickly enough.

Sometimes unmerited praise can have serious consequences. The danger is that the child will actually demonstrate unacceptable behavior in an attempt to balance the situation.

For weeks, I worried about a football player whom I was not reaching. I tried several forms of communication before I realized that he was a perfectionist and did not want praise for his performance until it met *his* expectation.

Finally, I began to limit my praise and to evaluate as honestly as possible. He began to perform at a higher level. Eventually, he could accept my praise because he was pleased with what he was doing.

4. Learn to like your child.

I didn't say *love* him. I said *like* him. Develop a friendly rapport. This is different from trying to be his buddy or to be ten years old again. That is a mistake. But develop lines of communication so the two of you don't feel awkward about being in each other's presence. You may have to work at this, but it can be accomplished.

When I was in school, I befriended a fellow student who had developed a pattern of running away from home. Since he came to our house each time, I found myself involved in his family dispute. Finally, counselors suggested a more wholesome relationship between the father and son—spending time together, doing the kinds of things both liked to do.

Consequently, one fall I spent every Saturday accompanying the pair on hunting trips. It was the most discouraging period of my life. The two were together, all right—in the same way Custer and the Indians were together at Little Big Horn. The father would yell instructions at the son. The son would refuse to obey. The father would then question the son's mental ability. The son would question the father's right to authority. The father would yell back, the son would pout, and the bird population remained unharmed. By the end of the day, all of us were in tears.

Actually, the counselors had not given bad advice; they had just given incomplete advice. These two needed to learn to like each other. Without this as a purpose, those hunting trips only contributed to the gaps and the scars.

5. Don't feel that you have to provide a conscience for your child.

I am always surprised by parents who act shocked when their children spill something during a meal. This is one of the occupational hazards of parenthood. You may as well anticipate it.

If you bring your six year old to my house for dinner, he will probably spill food. This in no way reflects on his ancestry or intelligence. I have never seen a child spill food intentionally. I have never seen one spill food without feeling guilty about it. I have never seen a child spill food without being embarrassed. If your child spills food at my table, you should not feel obligated to correct his moral depravation at that moment.

As adults, most of us know the feeling of uttering something for which we are immediately sorry. We wish we could take the comment back, and we appreciate the people who pretend to ignore it. During those moments, our own guilt is sufficient.

If your son strikes out with the bases loaded, he probably knows what he has done. The image is vivid in his mind. He doesn't need your help to relive his unforgettable moment.

A Sense of Belonging

As I followed the unfolding of the tragic story of Jim Jones and the People's Temple, I became impressed with the innate human need to belong and with the measures some people will take to fulfill that need. I also became impressed with the possibility that there are millions who are searching for something to belong to. Everyone needs someplace to go when he can't go anywhere else. The family is the most obvious answer to that need, but apparently it isn't working that way.

The schools have tried to compensate with various kinds of programs designed to stimulate loyalties. A good school is one that thrives on something called school spirit. A good school is one in which the students can feel they belong. This kind of community spirit doesn't happen by accident. It is usually planned and engineered by an astute staff; and for some students, it fills a big vacuum.

But there are some dangers in having schools fulfill this need. A student can't stay in school all his life. It saddens me to see a student who has developed such loyalty to his high school that he can't find identity after he graduates. Frequently, this happens to people with promise and ability. Some find a degree of satisfaction by taking a position as a custodian or member of the staff. Others just loiter, searching for the glory, the sense of belonging, the success and acceptance that was high school to them.

Another problem is that the schools can't reach everyone. Thus, wise parents do not depend on the schools to give their children a sense of belonging. This is, in fact, one of the valuable roles of your family life—to provide each member, regardless of how old he is, with a sense of belonging. Again, it may not come naturally. You may have to work at it. Because of this I offer the following five suggestions.

1. Be consistent.

It is easy to to express happiness with a child who has just made the honor roll or has sung a beautiful solo in church. It is easy to be a parent when the child is happy and successful. But who is going to be your child's parent when he does something that embarrasses you and even himself? Who is going to be his parent when he is dealing with drunkenness or pregnancy? Who is going to be your child's parent when he has the greatest need for a parent?

Your child really doesn't need you in the midst of his success; others are accepting him then. He needs you most when there are no other people to accept him. Are you prepared for that?

You may protest, "My child won't come home with the problem of drunkenness or pregnancy." That may be true, and I hope it is. But your child is going to do something against your wishes. You can depend on it. There is just a difference in degree. Who is going to love your child (and who is going to express that love) when he is disobedient?

While I was a principal, our basketball team played at a neighboring school. During the game, two of our student spectators practiced their high-jumping skills in a remote corridor of the building. In the process, they damaged several ceiling tiles. The following day, I rounded up the boys, called their fathers from their jobs, and charged the families with the responsibility of restitution. Since the fathers worked at different ends of town, I held a separate conference for each family.

The difference between the two was overwhelming. One father came quickly. He raved to the son about responsibility, upbringing, family embarrassment, and inconsideration. Finally, exhausted and exasperated, he said to his son, "I don't want anything to do with you. This is your doing. You'll have to get out of it the best you can. I'll take you home to your mother." And with that, they left.

The other father was more poised. He explained to his son, in a firm but mild voice, the embarrassment and the hurt. Then he explained that just as the child would suffer in the event of the father's poor judgment, the father would suffer for the son's poor judgment. Together, they traveled to the other town to correct the mistake.

Christian parents have a mandate of love. Our children must be able to depend on the constancy of that love, consistent through the bad times and the good. We must provide them with an understanding climate for confession, repentance, and restoration. Our Lord has done that for us, and we are commanded to do that for our children.

2. Don't be afraid to correct your child.

Don't confuse accepting your child with neglecting to correct him. Your child doesn't confuse them. Every day I encounter parents who are afraid to approach their children about some misbehavior for fear the child may respond with hate and hostility. That is a blatant mistake. Children can be corrected, should be corrected, *must* be corrected. They may object for a while, but they will recover. The real danger is in ignoring the misbehavior.

As an educator, I have frequently encountered a student who has undergone a sudden, unpleasant change of behavior. He has done some things that have embarrassed him and the people who depend on him. When I call the child in to get to the root of the matter, I discover that he has been guilty of some rebellious act. He feels that his parents know and should correct him. But until he is corrected, he must continue the rebellious pattern.

In his mind he is socially unacceptable until he has paid for his sin. In simple terms, he is in dire need of a parental demonstration of love through correction. This is especially common in children of Christian parents, because the children have a strong sense of right and wrong.

But there is a right way to correct. Always deal with the act and not with the person. I realize that this is almost a cliché, so let me give a specific example. One of the most meaningless utterances in rearing children is the question, *Why?* I suppose its use generates from a strange American misconception that every question has one simple, correct answer. Parents seem to believe that if we yell that question loud and often, the child can give us one terse, correct, comprehensible, brief reason for the most complex of human activities.

Be specific. Tell the child what he has done. Explain to him that it was wrong, bad judgment, a mistake. Point out to him why he can't do such things again. When he understands, work out a suitable punishment which will remind him not to make the same mistake. And for good measure, hug him after your talk. But whatever you do, *correct him*. Children with good parents expect it.

This whole business of punishment, and particularly suitable punishment, is a tricky one. Some parents who are otherwise thoughtful and sensitive seem to catch a severe case of "stone minds" when it comes to thinking of a punishment suitable to the crime. The first impulse is to hit. Since the seat has become the depository of moral decision making, it usually seems the likely location.

However, the impulse to hit is probably first because it is the most primitive. The ancient Spartans bit the child's thumb. That makes more sense since the thumb is one of the things that distinguishes man from animal. At least, they attacked something human. (I correct my *dog* by hitting him on the seat.)

Parents who control the urge to hit still may not have mastered the secret of proper punishment. Too many resort to one form, and when one form of punishment is used too frequently it loses its effectiveness. Grounding your child is an appropriate punishment when he has violated his right to free movement, but doesn't work for every parental frustration you are ever going to have. Not permitting him to have guests over is appropriate when he has not cleaned his room. Making him find and write new vocabulary words is appropriate when he has used bad language.

3. Permit your child emotional experimentation.

After having been married more than two decades, I am beginning to understand my wife. One of the things I now know is that she cannot have a good day every day. Sometimes I come home in the evening and greet her with a loving and tender gesture. She responds with a brusque, "Hang up your coat." I am willing to accept that response from her. She is under a lot of pressure. She has responded with emotional honesty. She doesn't hate me, and home should be the place where she can be honest.

Yet, when one of my children practices the same kind of honesty, I may yell, shout, stomp, bare my teeth, and show my authority. But children have the same needs as my wife. They need a place where they can be honest with their emotional status. They also need to experiment with emotions.

One definition of maturity is knowing how to respond emotionally to a given situation. Immature people can't become mature unless they can experiment. Your child may say to you, "I hate you," and it may be a fairly accurate appraisal of his feeling at that point. But don't let it disturb you all that much. It may even be a mistake to try to reason him out of it. Just demonstrate through your consistency that you really don't deserve that particular emotion, and he will soon try another.

4. Don't hold grudges, but finish ugly situations as soon as possible.

Never forget that you are the adult in the relationship and you should be more skilled in the art of forgiving than your child is. Start the relationship anew on happy terms as quickly as possible.

Respect for Authority

In recent years we have learned that society is not controlled by law. Rather it is controlled by respect for law. Laws alone will not prevent chaos, confusion, or violence. Someone must respect the laws and the people who enforce the laws.

A local school district built a new building about ten years ago. In the middle of the front foyer is a beautiful, inlaid bulldog, the school mascot. It soon became traditional not to walk on the bulldog. Although there are no signs, no barricades, and no ropes, students do not walk on the bulldog. During the exchange period, the hall is filled with hurrying students, but all step around the bulldog. Students avoid the bulldog not because of rules or threats, but because of tradition.

Schools have laws, and school people assume that children come to school with a healthy respect for authority and a desire to live according to the law. If the children do not have this respect for law and order, then school laws and, subsequently, schools are powerless. About the only way the schools have of addressing such lack of respect is through force and coercion, and this approach teaches fear rather than respect.

To make the matter worse, your child's environment is filled with role models that contradict respect for authority. The public servants are corrupt, the police are dishonest, professional athletes argue with the officials, drivers cheat at tollgates—the list is endless. Yet the future of this country and the role your child will play in that future depend largely on his learning a healthy respect for authority. Here are a few suggestions to help you teach him.

1. *Teach the child a biblical world view.*

The Christian lives under the authority of God, and this authority gives the world unity, clarity, meaning, and value. The good life is one that is totally submitted to that authority.

Your child is not going to learn this lesson in school. If he is to learn it, you are going to have to teach it. If he doesn't learn it, you must accept the blame. Begin by having the child learn those Bible verses pertaining to the authority of God that is inherent in His majesty and genius.

Show your children role models who have found great happiness through being fully committed to God's authority. Make those role models heroes with the appeal of a professional basketball player. The Bible is filled with such stories. The biographies of Moses and Daniel are just two examples.

2. *Develop friendships with people who have authority over your child.*

Let the child see those authority figures as individuals. Invite teachers to your home. Stop and chat with a policeman when your child is present. Have a friendly conversation with a sports official.

3. *Accept authority yourself.*

Be a role model. Every time you criticize a referee, you do some damage to your child. Let your child know that you know the value of authority and are prepared to live with it.

4. *Never take your child's side in a situation until you have heard both sides.*

Again I am not saying *your* child lies, but some children do. If it pays off for them, they will probably develop a pattern of it. Just make sure you get all the evidence before you tackle the authority. Things may not be exactly as they were presented.

Some teachers, only half in jest, send a note home to parents suggesting a compromise: They won't believe the children's stories about home if the parents won't believe the stories about school. Think about it. You may want to initiate such an agreement with your child's teacher.

A Desire to Learn

We learn most quickly those lessons that are immediately applicable and valuable to our lives. Most lessons taught in schools have long-range values. Teachers talk about the importance of motivation in student success. Motivation comes from the student's ability to see the value of a lesson. Parents have a role, an important role, in helping their children see the long-range value to what they are presently doing. This point will be covered further in Chapter 8, but I offer a few specifics here.

1. *If you ridicule intellectualism, be ready to accept the consequence of your child becoming narrow and provincial.*

Be careful about saying such things as, "I don't know why he's making you learn that. I don't see where that will ever do you any good." "I never learned grammar in my life and look where I am now." And be particularly careful about evaluating learning with dollar marks in such statements as, "Garbage workers make more money than teachers." That's true, but you are helping your child develop a very important and possibly dangerous attitude when you point it out. Being a garbage worker is a noble choice of career, but no such decision should be based on dollars alone.

Just remember that great thinkers discovered the polio vaccine, developed electricity, and wrote Shakespeare's plays. Of course, there is a big difference between the pseudointellectual and the real one, and it may be your duty to point out the difference. But be careful that in your zealous efforts, you don't give all thought a bad name.

2. *Let your child see you study.*

You may have more success when you say, "Go do your homework," if your child frequently sees that you are involved with productive learning activities.

3. *Be interested in your child's academic work.*

Make schoolwork an important part of family life. Encourage him to talk about what he is learning and help him draw practical applications from those lessons.

If your child is to survive the process of growing up and reach adulthood with some capacity for happiness and love, he will need to have self-worth, a sense of belonging, respect for authority, and a desire to learn. School officials, if they are honest, will admit that they can't teach those lessons effectively. Despite all their noble attempts, the responsibility is yours. Your child must learn these basic lessons of life at home.

Educators frequently admit, "The more important the lesson, the more difficult to measure the outcome." That adage applies here. The attitudes discussed in this chapter are among the most valuable lessons you will ever teach your child. It is important for you to know how well you are doing. But since the lessons are so important, immediate measurement is difficult. By using the suggestions in this chapter and by maintaining a constant and caring relationship with your child, you can get a dim idea now. Twenty years from now, you will be able to see the results more clearly.

Homework Assignment for Parents

1. What specific things do you do repeatedly to build up your child's self-worth? What things, if any, do you do to damage it?

2. While "school spirit" helps a child to feel a sense of belonging at school, do you attempt any kind of "home spirit" to make sure he feels at home with his own family? And while doing so, do you continue to demand responsibility and respect on his part?

3. In what ways does your child show respect for authorities? In what ways is he an occasional rebel?

4. Does your child learn because he has to or because he wants to? How can you increase his desire? What things do you do to indicate to him that the learning process never ends?

8

Parents and Schools: Sharing the Responsibility

I used to interview prospective teachers for employment. These candidates were frequently just out of college with new diplomas, fresh certificates, and wholesome attitudes. This was during an era of teacher surplus, so each person felt a burning need to convince me that he or she was the world's greatest teacher—highly skilled, efficient, thorough, and compassionate.

Somewhere in the midst of the conversation, I would always ask, "How good were your college courses in education—teaching theory and methodology?"

Now that is a tricky question. Teachers everywhere love to sit for hours and criticize their college education courses. Many of these young candidates in my interview couldn't avoid the temptation. In glowing speeches they told me that the professors were bad, that the material was irrelevant, and that they had not learned anything.

As an educational administrator, I didn't want to hire people who by their own admission hadn't learned anything in their college courses. I wanted to hire people who went to good schools and learned about the art of teaching. I was amazed at how many young teachers fell into my trap and talked themselves right out of a job.

I feel the same amazement when I go to a party and listen to parents broadcast for hours about how stupid their own children are. Since I am considered an educator, parents love to tell me about their children's experiences in schools. Many proclaim how Suzy can't read, Johnny can't cipher, Billy can't spell, and Sally can't write.

Parents think they are impressing me with how bad schools are, but I already know what schools are doing. I visit schools every day. Instead, what I am learning from those critical parents is how bad parents are, or more specifically, how bad they are as parents.

Let's face reality. Regardless of what the school is supposed to be doing, regardless of how good or bad it may be, your child's ability or inability in such activities as reading, writing, and performing math skills is your concern. If your child is going to reach adulthood with proficiency in the basic skills of learning and living, *you* will have to help him learn them.

In fact, if your child is going to thrive and survive in school, you will sometimes have to supplement the classroom activities. You will have to assume some of the responsibility of teaching.

The Parent as a Teaching Supplement

Until about the time of the Civil War, all instruction in schools was one-to-one. The student sat in some corner of the classroom, usually with his back to the center, and studied from his text. When he had prepared his lesson (or had memorized the material), he went to the teacher's desk. There he recited as the teacher listened, prodded, and sometimes applied strong reminders with a switch. For thousands of children who lived prior to the mid-nineteenth century, this was school—a slow, prodding process built on the principles of memorization and recitation.

Eventually, more innovative teaching methods developed. The learning process became more exciting—more student-centered than content-centered, more experiment/interaction-based, and more group-oriented. Yet with all the virtues of these new techniques, the values of memorization and recitation have never been fully eliminated.

To become educated, children must learn some things that can only be mastered by committing facts to memory and repeating them so often that they became second nature. The contemporary classroom is not designed for efficient use of recitation, repetition, and memorization, nor is the contemporary teacher equipped to provide adequate time for those activities.

Most teachers simply have too many students and too little time. The average elementary class size is between twenty-five and thirty-five. A typical school day is approximately 330 minutes. A minimum of thirty minutes of each day is devoted to administrative procedures such as calling roll and collecting money.

Other important activities such as music and physical education take large blocks of the school day. With this limited time budget, the teacher must rely on group instruction for most of the learning. It is a rare privilege for a teacher to be able to spend a few precious minutes in a one-to-one relationship with a specific student.

Some students—the ones we call "bright"— can master material with a minimum amount of recitation and repetition. Others need supplementary help, and this is the role of the parents.

Reading

Reading is one example. Most reading specialists tell us that good readers begin their educational success story while they are still in the crib. Parents are encouraged to model good language in dealing with even the smallest infants, avoiding baby talk and meaningless speech patterns.

According to those same specialists, one of the best methods of promoting good reading skills is for the parents to read to the child. If you have started that practice, continue it even after the child starts school. The important point here is not the quality of the reading but the quality of the selections.

Pick something your child is interested in. Make your reading sessions a reward or a special time. Your preschool child may not comprehend all the subtleties of a good piece of children's literature, but he will surprise you. Promise your child that when he starts kindergarten, you will begin reading the *Narnia Chronicles*. Thus, he will have some positive expectations of both school and the activity of reading.

Listen to your child read. Beginning readers must read aloud. In the event your child's teacher is too busy, make yourself available. The kind of reading you do is a very complex activity; but at its most elementary level, reading is saying. Provide your child an audience to practice his reading at that level. Be careful not to be so critical that you take the joy out of it for the child; but at the same time, provide enough feedback for him to make corrections.

Good readers are people who have read a lot. There are no shortcuts. I have heard parents criticize teachers when their children cannot read, but this only labels the parent as a person who would rather seek excuses than assume parental responsibility. If you want your child to be a good reader, you will probably have to supplement his school lessons.

Arithmetic

Following Sputnik, some teachers introduced new ways to teach arithmetic and eliminate all the drudgery of memorization. The idea had appeal, but it was not totally accurate. Regardless of how many calculators you can afford to buy your child, he is still going to need to know the basic facts tables if he is ever going to function in society. And the only way to learn those tables is to memorize them.

Some students memorize the arithmetic facts rather easily. Some need more drill. Don't be ashamed of your child or critical of the school if your child is one of the latter. Drill him yourself.

We wallowed in the slough of despair over our daughter's arithmetic scores until we realized that we would have to supplement her school lessons. We made games of addition, subtraction, and multiplication facts, and we played those games at every opportunity—in the car traveling to Grandmother's house, during TV commercials, and in restaurants waiting for our food. Even the older siblings got involved. In a very short time her scores improved and her confidence went up.

Writing

Writing is a procedure for communicating ideas. Thus, if the writer is going to experience the purpose of writing, someone must read his material. The parent is the first candidate. (Of course, if the child does not want you to read his material, comply with his wishes. Some things are personal.) Again, you need to be aware of the balance between too little and too much criticism. The important thing is to be an available audience.

One night I worked at my office writing a manuscript. In the quiet, I had a burst of inspiration. My ideas came fast, my fingers worked obediently, and I finished the project. I literally ran home to share it with my wife. She read it and made some nice comments, but wasn't very enthusiastic. I was disappointed with her response until I realized that it was two o'clock in the morning, and she had been asleep for three hours.

But that night I realized the importance of having someone read my ideas immediately. Sometimes teachers cannot provide the immediate reaction your child's thinking deserves. You must provide it for him. He will learn to write, not through drill, but when he knows he is communicating.

The preceding examples are only that— examples. All through your child's educational career, he is going to need some help from you. Don't despair at the inadequacy of the school. Overcome it.

The Special Student

One fall a senior transfer student entered my British literature class. I had met this young man previously during a church activity, so I had some data about him. On the first day, I gave a rather simple assignment. As the others began to work, he came to my desk and reported that he could not do the assignment. When my face indicated doubt, he said, "Didn't they tell you? I'm dumb."

I ignored the statement and asked him if he could adjust the points on my automobile, a strange, German machine with obstinate tendencies. He asked a couple of technical questions I couldn't answer, then volunteered to go to the parking lot to see what he could do. I readily granted permission.

About thirty minutes later, he came back and reported that the car was running perfectly, following minor adjustment. I was then able to point out to him that he was, in fact, not dumb, but very intelligent. Although I had absorbed a lot of information, he had a skill and a gift. He had already contributed to my living a happier life, and I hoped I could return that favor.

I have never had a student who tried as hard or was more congenial. This young man is now a very happy, successful, automobile mechanic. He shows every indication of having overcome the attitude that God had cheated him in creation.

In His infinite wisdom, God created each of us to be different. It is not my intention to get into the awesome, complex, and sometimes confused field of special education. That is a study that deserves more than a few paragraphs. Rather, I want to mention those very select people whom God ordained to be more gifted with their hands than with words. They are not just valuable to our society; sometimes I think they are the backbone of it. They make my automobile safe, my house strong, my furnace warm, and my refrigerator cold. I suppose I respect them so much because I have absolutely no ability with my hands.

Yet, the public schools have never quite decided what to do with these very special people. If you are fortunate enough to be the parent of one, you are going to have to be especially sensitive to his or her needs. Education, as I perceive it and have described it throughout this book, is disciplining the mind in the use of symbolic language. Schools are necessary to teach people the language of thought. A person who is gifted with his hands may not always be successful in school. Through diligence and perseverance, he may master enough to get by; but he will never be a distinguished student.

Schools do provide special programs for these students—shop classes, vocational projects—but there is always a stigma attached. In people's minds these are programs for the low-ability students, the misfits, the potential dropouts. Educators will protest this statement, but they can't deny that the stigma exists in the minds of most students and most teachers—in fact, in the culture itself.

This stigma makes school especially difficult for the Christian student with special abilities. I suspect a self-fulfilling prophecy at work, but whatever the reason there are usually more smokers in these classes, more poorly motivated students, and more potential dropouts.

The Christian student who finds himself in this company will need a lot of love and support from his parents. He will need constant assurance that he is not a bad person because he doesn't get an A in history or is not planning an illustrious college career with a full academic scholarship. He will need to be reminded that his Savior was a carpenter, that Peter was a fisherman, and that Paul made tents.

If your child has a special gift, he will need your support. Make him feel that mechanics or carpentry (or whatever his particular skill) is a good field. Give him abundant opportunities to use his craftsmanship for you. Give him tools instead of books for presents. Make plans with him for the full development of his talent. Treat that development as you would a college education for another child.

The Importance of Knowing Your Child

I cannot anticipate or discuss all the classroom strengths and weaknesses in your child's academic growth. But if you use these examples as guides, you should be able to detect the early warning signs and create some kind of learning circumstance to help your child.

If you are still at a loss, consult a teacher. He is probably as disturbed about the problem as you, and he will want to help. Good teachers are interested in the same thing as you—your child's maximum development.

Actually, there is a hidden message in this chapter: You must have a good relationship with your child. I really didn't mean to hide the assumption, nor did I intend to trick you. But it is basic to this chapter, this section, and this book. Let's look at the thought progression.

If your child is going to succeed in school and in life, you must supplement his classroom instruction. To supplement the classroom instruction, you must detect deficiencies and possible problems. To detect such problems, you must have a close relationship with your child.

When the teacher wants to know the child's weaknesses, he sits him down and gives him a test. That is a little awkward for you. You must gather such evidence from frequent and meaningful conversations or from watching your child do his homework, play games, or read a book.

If your relationship is close enough for you to analyze your child's development, you have already begun the process of supplementation. In all teaching, the quality of the relationship between teacher and student is more important than the quality of the method of instruction.

Without this relationship between parent and child, the material in this section on family loses meaning. When you search for a family nucleus, when you teach your child the important lessons of life, when you supplement classroom instruction, your efforts are at the mercy of your attitude toward your child and his attitude toward you. I hope you two like each other.

The Family at Work: A Final Story

Recently, I traveled to Brazil to conduct professional workshops for teachers of missionary children. The presupposition that motivates such trips is that I know something about educating children and that I can share my information in such a way that the classroom teachers will be more effective.

In this context, two false feelings can develop. First, it is easy to build an exaggerated image of yourself and your ability. Second, it is also easy to build an attitude about "poor little missionary children" who are "deprived of a decent education because they have to get their schooling in such limited conditions."

During the week, I stayed in the home of a missionary family with four children. Prior to my coming, the children had decorated the house with bright, cheery signs that directed me to all the necessary spots such as my room, my closet, the bathroom, the shower button, the guest towels, and so on. As the days passed, I found that these children had anticipated every need; each time I wanted something there was a sign directing me. I surmised that we were either playing an interesting game, that these were exceptionally sensitive children, or that I am too predictable in my old age.

Each child had a pet, and each pet indicated no lack of love and attention. Even the parrot was bilingual. Breakfast was scheduled early enough to allow family Bible reading. Each person around the table took turns.

Part of the evening ritual included group reading of poetry and short stories and thoughts the family members had written during the day. There was also reminiscing about a family vacation they'd had about two months earlier.

Those children attend a school which probably wouldn't merit the educators' seal of approval. Teachers have to meet the awesome task of teaching multiple-level classes—as many as four different grade levels in the same classrooms at the same time. There are few library books and fewer magazines. Some of the textbooks are more than ten years old. The bathroom is a "down-the-path" variety. Frequently, the temperature inside the classroom exceeds 100 degrees. There is a limited curriculum, no overhead projector, no movie projector, and no videotaping equipment. Teachers frequently have to teach classes that are outside their area of preparation.

After watching these children for nearly a week, I concluded that the only things they had going for them were teachers who cared and a family life that worked. In all of my educational experience, I have never seen children as bright, happy, creative, and loving as those. Your children should be so deprived.

Homework Assignments for Parents

1. In what area(s) does your child need the most work (reading, writing, etc.)? If the school can't supply enough training in these areas, how can you make sure your child receives the attention he needs at home?

2. What talent(s) does your child have outside the traditional academic arena? (Is he better at mechanical repair than with writing stories? Does he want to be outside "building things" so much that you can hardly get him to do his homework?) Do any of his actions indicate an inclination for vocations other than white collar jobs? And if so, how can you help him develop in those areas that the school is likely to deemphasize?

3. Do you regularly check to see if your child is motivated in a specific direction? If not, how can you get to know him better and discover his true inner thoughts and feelings?

SECTION 3:
THE POWER OF
PEERS

9

Choosing Friends

W e never had any trouble with Brian. He was always a good boy, and he tried hard to please us. He was handy around the house. Oh, we had to nag him about chores sometimes, but he got them done eventually. He was a little better than average student—B's and C's. We always thought he could do better, but we didn't push him.

We did worry because he didn't have many friends. He never had kids over to the house, and he never went home with anyone. But it didn't seem to bother him much, so we didn't press the issue. He seemed to like being at home. We played a lot of games as a family. His father taught him chess, and they played almost every night.

A couple of times we tried to get him into some friendship-making activities. We tried Little League baseball, but Brian was so uncoordinated that he never got to play much. Since he spent most of his time sitting on the bench, we decided it wasn't worth his time or ours. We also tried Boy Scouts, but he just never seemed to get interested.

When Brian started high school, he announced that he wanted to go out for the hockey team. It seemed to be a good sign—a sign that he was moving out of his shell and into some social relationships.

We had never realized how irregular hockey practice was. Since the high school team couldn't get the rink at decent hours, they either practiced in the wee hours of the morning or really late at night. It wasn't easy, taking him to practice and being there to pick him up when it was over. We were pleased when he told us that some of the older boys had cars and could take him back and forth.

He was finally getting some socialization. It was true that he was gone from home a lot, and frequently stayed out late, but we assumed that he was practicing hockey all that time. He became more antisocial at home. He rarely entered into family games, and he spent a lot of time in his own room. He grew short-tempered. But we just decided that it was because of the irregular hours.

We never realized we had a problem until the night the police called. . . .

* * *

Charles was a stubborn child, almost from birth. By the time he was old enough to walk he was throwing regular temper tantrums. School didn't change him—it just spread his rebelliousness over a wider area. During his first three years in school, one of us had to go visit the teacher almost every week.

He was never into anything really bad—just acts of defiance. He wanted to manage his own affairs and he didn't welcome too many suggestions, whether they came from us, from teachers, or from the other children. He was probably a bully, but I never admitted it.

He was not dumb, but because he was so rebellious, he never did very well in school. Every time he had homework, we had to force him to do it, and then he did everything with such a flippant attitude.

Secretly, we shuddered when we heard reports of problems other people were having with their teenagers. We weren't managing Charles in elementary school. What were we in for when he got to high school? We were doing the best we could—church and Sunday school, activities, family trips—but we weren't seeing much progress.

When he was in the eighth grade, Charles discovered wrestling. He had tried sports before, but never with much success. He was just too much of an individual. He was always in trouble with his coaches. But wrestling was different. The two seemed to have been made for each other. Almost immediately we began to see a difference. For one thing, he was an instant success. He won with regularity. He began to invite his wrestling friends over after practice. He worried about his diet. At the coach's urging, he began to take his classwork more seriously. He was genuinely pleased when the family came to his matches. He became cooperative and even a bit affectionate.

He breezed through high school with good grades and a good attitude. He won wrestling awards by the dozens, but he also won other awards for scholarship and citizenship. Now Charles is in college on a wrestling scholarship and is still winning matches and friendships. What a change that one activity made in our son's life!

Those two opening stories are fictional, but could easily be true. Any person who has counseled parents for any length of time has a warehouse of such examples. The problem lies in the conflicting outcomes. Why did an extracurricular activity save one fellow and do the other in?

There is nothing inherently evil in hockey or inherently good in wrestling. Nor are the people in those two sports good or bad. The answer to the contradiction lies deeper than this.

From dozens of real-life examples just like my two fictional ones, we can conclude that peer activities and peer relationships are among the strongest factors in determining a child's approach to himself and the art of living. But we can also conclude that there is no guarantee about the kind of influence these relationships will have. Some are positive; some are negative; some are even destructive.

Here is the dilemma. Your child's selection of friends and activities could have a tremendous influence on the kind of adult he becomes, on the kind of life he lives and endorses, on the kind of beliefs and ambitions he holds. Yet, it is almost impossible to anticipate what the outcome of a given activity or friendship will be.

For these reasons, the next few chapters could be the most important section in this book. As I have tried to deal with friendships, extracurricular activities, and the "terrible three" (drugs, sex, and alcohol), I have struggled with this dilemma myself. I have even proposed some suggestions for you, but I make these suggestions with the reservation that I cannot predict outcomes. What your child brings to, or needs from an activity or friendship will affect what he gets from it. For you to know what he brings to any situation, you will have to know your child. Please read this section with that in mind.

Know Your Child's Friendship Needs

During the growing process, children need loving parents and caring teachers, but they also need friends—people from their own peer group who can be a mirror, a sounding board, and a companion in joys and heartaches.

Your child's selection of friends will be a significant factor in determining the patterns of his youth. Choosing friends is among the most important decisions he will make, yet you are almost powerless to help him. In fact, the more conspicuous any attempts at intervention, the more futile are your efforts.

Don't bother asking your child why he chose his friends. He doesn't know why. There isn't much rationality involved in childhood friendships.

One preschool-age boy will walk through the toys of the boy next door to go farther down the street to play. Two youngsters will fill all their waking hours together either playing or fighting—extremes at both ends—but they are friends. Two high school students begin to date, and the teachers' lounge buzzes with "What does she see in him?"

School provides your child with a variety of types from which to select friends. This diversity can be a very wholesome thing. It can serve as both an educational agent and a ministry. You do need to be alert to the kind of friendships your child is making, but you also need to be very subtle in pressuring the child either into or away from a given relationship.

Perhaps the first thing you need to do is to conduct a little amateur psychological analysis. Study your child objectively. Understand how he operates within a friendship.

Is your child a follower or a leader? If he plays both roles depending on the relationship, ascertain what conditions determine which role he plays. In most friendships, there is a dominant and a recessive force.

Watch your child when he is with a friend. Who decides what games are played? Who enforces the rules? Who sets the standards of dress or hairstyle? Is your child more comfortable with quiet, nonaggressive children or does he get into relationships where the other person is dominant? Does your child prefer relationships with people his own age? Younger? Older? Does your child operate best with one very close friend at a time, or is he comfortable with a stable full?

One-to-one relationships between children are tender. They are sometimes built on possessiveness and partial "blindness." Children who hurl themselves into a singular relationship will inevitably be hurt. They will need a lot of love and family nurturing during moments of despair.

The first impulse is to teach this kind of child how to have several friends so that one won't matter that much. But that is contrary to his psychological makeup. Just be prepared to minister to him.

All these questions are keys for understanding your child's friendship needs. Study them carefully. If you are convinced that you have appropriately taught your child the difference between right and wrong, you must further acknowledge that his ability to fulfill that teaching is largely dependent on his role in the friendship.

It takes a tough kid to back out of the action and go home when he realizes he shouldn't be there. It is virtually impossible to get out of a speeding car while it is in motion. If your child is a follower, you will need to teach him now to get out of a situation before it gets out of hand. If your child is a leader, intensify the teaching of appropriate behavior.

Binding Agents

I have already pointed out the futility of trying to control your child's choice of friends. But there are some general trends which may help you understand certain allegiances.

Classroom Performance

One of the strongest attractors among all ages of schoolchildren appears to be classroom performance. Good students select their friends from other good students. Average students relate to average students. Low achievers gravitate to other low achievers.

This is evident even with a tightly knit activity. Football players usually associate with other football players, but their friendships are not based *only* on athletic ability. If a young man is a star athlete and a good student, then his friends will probably be from the team, but they will be the other good students on the team.

Activities and Clubs

Activities and clubs are natural adhesives, because they unite people of common interests and force the participants to spend time together. Usually, we like people if we spend enough time to get to know them.

In fact, this strategy isn't bad for adults. If I am having difficulty liking someone, I make a point to spend more time with him. Soon the barriers go down and the friendship goes up. Friendships develop through before-school car pools, practice sessions, bus trips, and common frustrations and joys.

This is where parents can have some influence on friend selection. You can encourage participation in a certain activity by committing yourself to it. You may have to drive in the car pool rotation, and you will definitely have to wait dinner occasionally. Of course, you have the task of deciding which school activity attracts the kind of people you want for your child's friends. Somewhere, sometime, every parent is just going to have to trust the judgment of the child and claim God's name for divine direction.

Some Christian organizations operate in conjunction with the public schools. In some places they actually operate within the schools themselves. Some administrators welcome the staff members into the building during school hours. As one principal explained his reason to me, when the Christian club became active in his school, the vandalism costs diminished by several thousand dollars a year. With him it was sheer economics, but still it isn't a bad testimony as to what such an organization can do.

It might seem that such a club provides the perfect home base for the students from Christian homes, but there is also the danger of its becoming a Christian clique. Cliques are almost always detrimental to a school's overall program, and a Christian clique is a particular nuisance. I favor friendships among Christian students, but these young people must guard against closing the membership, lest they damage a person and the name of the One whom they serve.

The Church

The church provides the appropriate setting for children to develop relationships with other people who approach life through a faith in the freeing authority of God. Because of the Christian's ability to understand this paradox and to find happiness within it, these friendships can be very strong and rewarding. Parents who are concerned about the kinds of friendships their children make should take responsibility to see that their children attend educationally sound and socially conducive Sunday schools.

A problem with these church associations arises when the children in church are not from the same school. This can present a real conflict for the young person who is trying to develop some friendship ties. There is the appeal to commit himself to someone from church to get the value of a common faith and life-style. But there is also the appeal to commit himself to someone in school because he spends a greater portion of his time there.

The apparent solution is for the family to attend church in the neighborhood where the children all go to the same school. The strongest, most loyal, most productive, and most valuable friendships I have ever seen have been those where the children attended both the same church and the same school. When this is not possible, the family will have to supplement.

Some Problem Areas

If your children are in public school, you can expect to encounter specific problems concerning friendships. The rest of this chapter will discuss some problem areas you should be aware of.

Questionable Special Events

I endorse the role of strong family relations, but there are times when young people need to be with their peers instead of their family. The postgame celebration party is a time for young people to relax and play together. The post-graduation party is a time for the graduates to be together. The purpose of school dances and proms is not to promote dancing, but to provide opportunities for fellowship and social inter-actions.

Children need these times together. They serve a valuable role in the process of maturation, and no parents want to deprive their child of peer relationships. The child is not renouncing his family just because he wants to be with people his own age during those times.

However, some of those parties may not be something you want your child to attend. They may include activities that you can't condone—drinking, dancing, or public displays of affection. How do you permit your child the opportunity for social development without sacrificing your standards?

The answer lies in substitution, but it isn't easy to accomplish. If you are concerned about this part of your child's environment, you are going to have to initiate some effort. It's up to you to hold some social events of your own.

I once taught in a small town where the best postgame party was at the First Baptist Church. Other groups sponsored some sock hops and dances. But when the young people (particularly the players) flocked to the church party, the other parties soon disappeared. It took effort, but those church mothers were concerned enough to make it work.

If you can't get your church interested in hosting fifty hungry and rowdy students for meaningful fellowship, open your home. You might be surprised at the success. Don't worry about the appearance of the house. Your guests won't even notice the worn carpet or peeling paint if they sense they are welcome there.

The "Picked-on" Kid

I define prejudice as the seemingly inherent human need for someone to feel superior to another person. People in Kansas tell Okie jokes; the people in Oklahoma tell jokes about the dumb Arkansan; and the people in Arkansas tell jokes about stupid people from Louisiana. Distinctions may be ethnic, economic, regional, occupational, or religious, but the motivation is always the same. At school, a few children at the bottom of the social heap will always bear the prejudices of all classes above them.

Occasionally Christian children are the victims. They may be verbally abused, socially excluded, and even physically attacked. Dealing with this problem requires a lot of parental maturity. Caring for our children is a basic instinct, and assisting them against their attackers is part of that care. But the first rule is: Don't overreact. Once you have mastered this, you are prepared to take one of several courses of action which may or may not be successful.

If your child is being picked on excessively, realize that the hatred which leads to the abuse is neither learned from nor condoned by the school or the school personnel. Don't delay. Tell the teacher what is happening. If he seems uncomfortable, he is probably only embarrassed because he had not discovered the problem himself. Attacks leading to physical abuse can be stopped. Name-calling and exclusion are different matters, but the teacher can use his position to counteract the attitudes that are causing the problem.

Don't be afraid to confront the parents of other children involved, but do so with a wholesome purpose. In a Chicago suburb, some young men under the influence of drugs jumped from their car and attacked another student who was walking home from school. He was subsequently hospitalized with some rather serious injuries. That evening the parents, learning the identity of the attackers, went to their homes. There, those Christian people witnessed to entire families about the power of God to redeem lives, and they gave the message credibility by practicing the art of forgiveness.

Don't deny your child the right to a full measure of human experience, including suffering (particularly when you can help him through it). Loneliness is a part of life. Enduring criticism, whether deserved and undeserved, is also part of life. I am not suggesting we abandon our children, but I am saying that there is a point up to which criticism will contribute to the maturing process.

The Non-Christian Friendship

There is no need for despair if your child chooses some friends from non-Christian homes.

He has valid reasons, and such friendships can promote good opportunities for a two-way ministry.

These friendships can teach your child the true meaning of the Christian experience. It is always good to realize that there are nice people outside the church. The distinguishing characteristic of the Christian is salvation through the grace of Jesus Christ—not merely a set of given behaviors. If you have taught your child well, he will maintain his standards. This is particularly important when your child begins to date a non-Christian.

The "My Sad Story" Cult

I must conclude this section with a strong warning to Christian parents about the young person who has learned to manipulate innocent people through the use of "My Sad Story." This person has some major problem—a bad home life, a learning disability or some other flaw, or perhaps a rough past with drugs, alcohol, or sex.

In some cases the story may be true. But often a person will use his situation to control a friendship. Christian young people are particularly susceptible because they are experimenting with the emotions and complexities of charity and service. Innocent and noble, they get caught up in a situation that brings unhappiness, tears, and despondency. It can drain them emotionally, and Christian commitment becomes a psychological trap rather than the beautiful and liberating experience it should be.

My-sad-story-tellers can manipulate and dominate the life of the one who is trying to help. Occasionally the teller feels that the story is losing its power, and punches it up by slipping into a past foray into "sin."

Christian young people are servants, but they aren't psychologists. Parents must help them realize when they are being used. This so-called "friend's" expectations may go beyond boundaries of decent behavior.

A Glimmer of Hope

Since the days when Stoics and Epicureans roamed the streets of ancient Athens, the characteristics and attributes of friendship have been a mystery, never quite submitting to scientific investigation or logical reasoning. As a parent, you may have a strong desire to end all that mystery surrounding your child's choice of associates. But you probably won't.

The next chapter on extracurricular activities may offer some suggestions on how to direct your child's interaction with certain kinds of people, but those suggestions aren't foolproof. Your child is still enough of an individual to be somewhat unpredictable.

Since this business of selecting friends is such a chancy affair, your hope lies in the thesis of this section. Make sure you have a workable relationship (dare I say friendship) with your child—a relationship that you have built by spending time with him. Then you will be in a position to understand the process—and perhaps even minimize some of the risks—when your child begins to make new friendships that will influence his present and his future.

Homework Assignments for Parents

1. How well do you know your child's friends? Do you trust him to make wise decisions in all of his relationships? If you have doubts, what are some ways you can try to make sure he feels the freedom to make good choices?

2. Is your child more of a leader or a follower within friendships? What are some specific pros and cons that you've noticed so far? What are some other things that you haven't yet noticed, yet are concerned about?

3. Do you give your child plenty of freedom to be with his friends without your presence? Make a mental list of places you could trust him with a group of other friends, and then give him some chances to "solo." (If you are exceptionally brave, let him host a big event for his friends after a game or on some other special occasion.)

4. When your child is picked on at school, what are some things you can do to lift his spirits? What are you doing to make sure he isn't guilty of picking on others?

10

The Extracurriculars

A good extracurricular program is one that has a place and a need for every student in school. Most schools, particularly high schools, provide extracurricular experiences in music, drama, debate, newspaper and yearbook editing, student government, literary projects, science clubs, and chess clubs as well as sports. Schools spend a large amount of money on these programs, so they apparently feel the activities have educational value.

Research supports this. Students who take an active role in extracurricular activities usually do better in the classroom. They have better attendance records, are involved in fewer discipline problems, and achieve higher grades.

Positive Side of Extracurricular Involvement

In addition to the educational value, there are a number of reasons why Christian students and parents should consider active and consistent participation in some school-sponsored, extra-curricular program. These programs can provide a benefit both to the student and to the parent and can help each get maximum value from the school experience.

1. *Extracurricular programs keep a student busy.*

I hate to use that old cliché, but idleness is an enemy to wholesome youth. Except in extreme cases, every young person has several hours each week to either waste or invest. Learning wrestling countermoves or banging cymbals in the marching band may not seem like much of an investment, but it beats shoplifting, streetwalking, or knuckle cracking.

Of course, there are liabilities as well. The time commitments sometimes infringe on such activities as homework and church participation. Wise parents will help their child make choices and budget time according to those choices.

2. *Extracurricular programs offer the most appropriate setting for teaching some very worthwhile lessons.*

Some of the lessons which rank high on both the educators' and parents' lists of educational expectations are difficult to teach. These lessons may be simple to verbalize but almost impossible to evaluate in practice. Good extracurricular programs sponsored by thoughtful coaches can provide a setting conducive to learning. Let me provide some examples.

A sense of self-worth—A student can become an important person through participation in one of the extracurricular programs. Of course, sports have a higher visibility and more hero status, but a student is more likely to discover something he likes about himself in the science fair than in the science class.

Perhaps I am making a case for the role of competition in building self-image. I have too many firsthand illustrations of how a young person's life can change when he identifies with some competitive program and achieves some success through it. I have seen drastic turnabouts, the immediate redirection of an entire life-style.

Maybe this has been more common in my career because I was in smaller schools where we had greater need of every person. Frequently, I had the opportunity to work with a student who had transferred from a larger school where he had been inconspicuous. We would put him to work, not by design but because we needed him. His entire educational career, and frequently the whole emphasis of his life, would change.

Grateful parents often thought we were better teachers, but that wasn't true. We just had a greater need of their child. And since we needed him for football and band, he was also there for English literature and algebra. This does make a case for small schools, but I will refrain from arguing it here. Despite the size of the school, your child can get involved somewhere. That involvement might help him realize that he was created with a purpose.

The value of teamwork—Frequently, success in an activity demands a certain amount of selflessness. The student must discipline himself to fit into a broader scheme. He may want to go off on some musical trip of his own, but he knows that will destroy the quality of the entire arrangement. He must play the notes in front of him if the orchestra is to sound good. He must learn to find happiness in the whole rather than in his individuality. He must cooperate.

Early in my career, I had the opportunity of coaching against a man who was already a legend. He had been synonymous with football in that small town for more than a quarter of a century, and his reputation portrayed him as a man of integrity and honor. When we played his team, I realized that the truth of the legend was revealed in every aspect of the game. His players were well-schooled, intense, competitive, and courteous. Playing his team was one of the privileges of my coaching career.

A few years later, I became acquainted with a young, popular surgeon who had grown up in that small town and had played for "Coach." The surgeon told me this story.

Coach had fallen ill and was in the hospital preparing himself for death. The surgeon went to visit. They filled nearly an hour reminiscing. When the visit ended, the doctor started to leave. Coach called him back and, in the quiet of that hospital room, made one final observation.

"Son," he said, "your hair is too long."

The popular, busy surgeon reported that he did not return to his office. He didn't even call in. He went straight to the barbershop, because when

Coach says your hair is too long, you get it cut. This is the kind of teamwork that can be gained from good coaching—from good extracurricular programs.

If you remember the opening illustration of this book, you may wonder why I rebelled at asking a player to cut his hair. This coach could tell my friend to cut his hair after having taught him for years. But in my case, the father wanted me to *begin* my program with that kind of legislation. The difference in relationship marks the difference between good and bad education.

Rewards of hard work—Talent is a reality. Some people are more naturally gifted in specific areas. Yet, in most extracurricular activities, a student can improve through hard, consistent training. A person with limited ability can make himself functional, and the talented participant can move toward his potential only through dedication.

In contemporary society, it is a rare privilege to encounter the joy of physical exhaustion that comes from having done one's best. Every child should have that privilege at some time.

I frequently attend high school sports banquets. Invariably, when the coach begins to distribute awards and accolades, there is a special recognition for some nonathletic-looking player who, through hard work, has made himself an important part of the team's success. The coach's comments include such phrases as "dedicated," "intense," "sacrifice," "total release," "above and beyond"; and the presentation is always followed with a large measure of sincere applause.

Importance of following the rules—Although all programs work in relationship to rules, the most conspicuous rules are seen in sports. A good coach teaches the athlete to play by the rules for the maximum enjoyment of everyone. If your child's coach teaches something else, reread the rules in Chapter 4 and plan a visit.

3. *Extracurricular activities provide an opportunity for community, both for the student and the parents.*

Most students join a particular community when they begin to participate in an extracurricular activity. One common practice is to make generalizations about participants in various programs: Debaters wear horn-rimmed glasses and carry briefcases. Wrestlers are always dieting. Musicians have soft muscles and bruises on their lips. Baseball players have tobacco stains on their teeth.

While such labeling isn't always accurate, there *are* some general tendencies within each group. That is why it is important for your child to spend some time and thought on his decision to join one of these particular communities. By nature of talent, he will probably have a link to these people, and he will grow closer through association.

The most wholesome approach to a community is interaction. Your child will be altered or directed or influenced by the community, but he will also contribute to it. He will find his identity and individuality by being a part of something.

Because of your child's choice of activities, you will spend time with a given set of parents. If your son plays football, you will probably get acquainted with some football parents. If your son blocks so their son can run, you will have a natural affinity. With a bit of effort on your part, you can have a positive influence on the direction of the group of school parents.

Occasionally, these relationships are formalized through parent organizations. Become a member of these groups. Not only will you be in a better position to support your own child, but you can be an asset to the organization.

4. *Extracurricular activities provide an opportunity for Christian witness.*

Although this point depends on the strength of the community and your effectiveness within it, both you and your child can find ample opportunity to witness to the majesty of God's saving grace through participation in a specific program. If you are accepted in the group and are not overbearing in your approach, you will probably find a very receptive crowd.

Talk with your child about this opportunity. Extracurricular participation should never require him to sacrifice his religious training or enthusiasm in order to be accepted. The community may need him to speak out against practices that are not in keeping with the Christian life-style.

One young Christian athlete went to his coach and complained about the profanity on the football field. The coach admitted his negligence and took immediate action. He called a team meeting, apologized for his use of profanity, and decreed that in the future no one would resort to that language. The team applauded the decision.

I know it is not a case of eternal salvation, but at least a group of men became aware of one young man's commitment to the Word of God.

5. *Extracurricular activities provide some children with a necessary release from pressure.*

Some children simply don't know how to play or how to relax. They are intense, serious, and businesslike. For the parent, this may not be the blessing it appears to be. Pressure and stress are enemies of good health, regardless of age. If your child fits into this pattern, teach him to play. Youth is too precious to be wasted on imitation adulthood. Your children have a lifetime to be serious.

Stress diseases and reactions—ulcers, mononucleosis, suicides—are prominent among the nation's children. Help your child find a diversion. If he is not motivated to do so, make an effort to promote it. These conscientious, dedicated children are real joys, but don't deprive them of their natural youth.

Potential Pitfalls of Extracurricular Involvement

It's always possible to get too much of a good thing. Extracurricular participation is no exception. Some warning signs are very obvious. We parents all know them. But we need someone to remind us occasionally. Let me offer you the list I use to remind myself of how I should respond to my children's participation.

1. *Don't let the child get into too much.*

This is a common tendency for a particularly talented child. Some are gifted in everything, and sponsors of various activities put pressure on students. This can only damage your child. It will give him guilt feelings he doesn't deserve.

Keep in mind that the state track meet will probably be on the same weekend as the state music festival. (Sometimes I suspect there is a federal law requiring that coincidence.) If your child is good at both activities, there will be a conflict. The only way to avoid that conflict is to make a decision earlier. Anticipate those conflicts before the pressure is put on your young child.

2. *Be prepared for total immersion.*

Sometimes a student throws himself completely into his extracurricular project. Some programs demand that much time. Musicians have to practice, athletes have to stay in shape, debaters have to research, actors have to memorize—all this effort takes time and can be upsetting.

Grades may go down. Family life may suffer. Church participation may be kept at a minimum. At this point, the child needs your wisdom in weighing the assets and liabilities. Does the value of the program justify its cost? Remember that idols come in various forms.

3. *Don't put unrealistic pressure on your child to succeed.*

Every parent wants a star. But your child's happiness is the primary goal. If your child is happy with his bench-sitting contribution, accept it. He probably has a better understanding of the situation than you, anyway.

4. *You cannot relive your life through your child.*

You have already been through childhood and adolescence. You can't reenter it. Don't project your ambitions, your desires, your goals, or your need for thrills onto your child. Accept what your child is and what he does.

5. *Make your child's participation a big deal.*

You don't have to overinflate his ego, but provide support. Make his band concert an important event, not because of the quality of his playing but because he is your child. Watch him play his athletic contests, even if he is not the star. Make the *child* important, rather than his accomplishment. That is doubly true if your child happens to be extremely good. Don't let him forget that his achievement is a gift from God, and it is his willingness to use that gift which is to be celebrated, not his success with it.

Regardless of your child's ability, a baseball bat or a brass trombone may be a reasonable investment in his efforts to survive adolescence and in your efforts to help him. At least, an interest in these things will give him some opportunity for peer association in a controlled environment (which *has* to be better than the unstructured peer association of the street-corner kind).

So when in the spirit of public interest, the television commentator asks, "It's six o'clock. Do you know where your child is?" you can smile and whisper, "Yeah. He's at basketball practice."

But don't shout lest someone hear you. Remember that participation in extracurricular activities is not necessarily a panacea designed to prevent all adolescent behavior. He will probably still act his age often enough.

Homework Assignments for Parents

1. How important are extracurricular activities to your child? Does he need more involvement? Or is he becoming too committed to them?

2. How does school size affect your child's involvement? If he is engulfed in a large school, are you helping him locate groups where he can learn to exercise his gifts, do what he likes to do, and develop a sense of teamwork? If not, list some possibilities that are open to him and see if he shows an interest.

11

The Big Three: Drugs, Sex, and Alcohol

Hesitantly, I introduce this chapter with a brief description of the nature of human values and value formation. The discussion is pertinent, as your child's relationship to these three "sins of the body" is indeed a question of values. But I don't want to leave the impression that these three areas represent the total of human values. No! In order for us to discuss values adequately, we would need to go a great deal beyond one's response to the temptations of drugs or alcohol. In fact, these things might, in some cases, be treated as symptoms. The value problem could be much deeper and more complex.

To simplify this discussion, it helps to think of a value as a boundary or a limit. In every moral human being there is some behavioral or social boundary that he will not, perhaps cannot, step over. We just can't allow ourselves to be out-of-bounds. Many of us like the risk of moving near the edge, but we can't step across.

In my career as an educator, I have met hundreds of young people who could never bring themselves to cheat on a test. There was a moral boundary that prevented them from taking a peek or carrying an answer into the test session. But these same young people who were so noble in testing sessions saw absolutely nothing wrong with copying someone's homework, word for word. Now explain that. On the one hand, these people had a moral conviction against cheating—they were actually incapable of cheating on a test. Yet they could copy homework without feeling guilty.

For a parent, the underlying questions as you read this chapter are: What are your child's values? What are his uncrossable boundaries?

A primary source for establishing boundaries is the authority figures in our lives. As a parent, your first concern with your child's value formation should be those figures. Who are the authority figures in his life? Yourself? Teachers? The Bible? Coaches? Sunday School teachers? Cool peers? Popular heroes? The minister?

I would like to think that there is inherent authority in some positions, such as that of parent or teacher. But the truth, I believe, is that every authority figure must first earn the right of authority.

In this book, I have related two experiences with coaches and haircuts. In the opening personal illustration, I had not earned the right to be an authority figure in the player's life. I could have exerted force, but forced response has little to do with value formation. On the other hand, the coach in the surgeon's story in Chapter 10 had earned the right to suggest short hair. In this case, if the coach valued short hair, the players also valued short hair.

Authority spreads to a person in two ways—by preaching and by example. One of the biggest sources of frustration in the lives of young people is the inconsistency between what adults say and what they practice. As you read this chapter, section by section, ask yourself this question, *Will I be satisfied if my child lives his life by the same principles that direct my life in response to drugs, sex, and alcohol?*

While you are thinking about the power of example in value formation, consider another point. Many of your child's daily influences demonstrate a life-style that takes a rather flippant attitude toward traditional morality. Most popular heroes don't endorse virtues such as abstinence and monogamy. TV programs, movies, and biographical accounts of famous people present, at best, a nonjudgmental attitude toward adultery and drunkenness. If your child is going to develop values contradictory to such models, you must work with his school to make that contradictory system appealing enough for him to establish his own personal boundaries.

Drugs

Drugs are a part of our society. They are about as prevalent as oxygen, and parents may as well accept that fact. Unless you lock him in the attic for the next fourteen years, he is going to have to make his own decision about what to do with drugs.

I know parents who have almost bankrupted themselves moving their families from one school district to another in searching for a drug-free school, but such a search is futile. Drugs are in inner-city schools. Drugs are in suburban schools. Drugs are in rural schools. Drugs are in public schools. Drugs are in Christian schools.

But not only are drugs in the schools, they are also in the factories and plants, the offices and stores, and the parties in the homes. We need to remember this. For some reason, there seems to be a certain kind of self-satisfaction for adults to think that the drug problem in this country is centered only in the schools. But this kind of thinking isn't profitable when it comes to solving the problem, and it may even be dangerous.

Today's generation of young people did not invent the drug problems in this culture. They are not the first to abuse recreational drugs. As parents and as citizens, we need to be concerned about the drug problem, but we need to realize that the problem is bigger than a few young people in the school system.

Actually, in recent years, there seems to be some indication that the problem of drug abuse is changing, if not improving a bit. From what I see and hear, drug use is now a little more localized, restricted to a specific group of students who tend to identify themselves in rather tight circles.

What this means to the average parent is to recognize that there are still drugs available and that your child will be confronted sometime with having to make a decision, but the pressure to use drugs may not be as pervasive as it was a few years ago. Some high school students tell me that they go months at a time in suburban schools without seeing any evidence of drug use, particularly in their circle of friends and classmates.

Nevertheless, we deceive ourselves in thinking that we don't have a problem, and wisdom demands that we prepare ourselves and our children to deal with what is happening.

The first question a parent must consider is why a young person would ever experiment with drugs, particularly considering the campaign of negative literature that has been conducted during the past several years. What would cause any young person ever to go against sound judgment and common sense to commit an act as risky as experimenting with any kind of recreational drug?

The answer to this is not easy. In fact, it is as complex as human life itself. I doubt that any of us ever understand fully the reasons for all our actions. Even the Apostle Paul had to struggle with the plight of doing what he shouldn't and not doing what he should. But for the sake of our own sanity as parents, let's propose some guesses.

1. *Peer pressure.*

You knew I was going to say that. Isn't this monster known as peer pressure the cause of almost all adolescent misbehavior as well as the cause of most parental anxiety? We all know that out there somewhere is a giant ogre named Peer Pressure just waiting to swallow all those innocent children. That all may be true, but peer pressure is a rather complex concept too.

Usually when we think of peer pressure, we visualize something overt—some loud-mouthed bully standing behind our child, taunting him with such challenges as, "You're chicken if you don't," or, "I dare you and I double dare you." This overt kind of peer pressure is a reality, and I am sure that some young people are even caught in this trap. But I doubt that this kind of challenge is the most widespread or the most powerful. Rather, I am more frightened by other more subtle kinds of peer pressure. We will look at several of these as separate topics.

2. *The need for stability and dependability in relationships.*

All of us need to feel that we belong and that someone loves us. We have a driving force within us to want to know exactly where we stand in relationship with the people closest to us. When those people closest to the teenager are his friends, then he is going to be subjected to a ton of peer pressure. To achieve or maintain status in the relationship, he may make some decisions or take some actions which go beyond his sense of moral boundaries.

This is a widespread problem. Most adolescents and pre-adolescents are rarely totally secure in relationships with their peers. This whole phenomenon of friendship at this age is too tenuous. For young people who are not secure in their relationships with their parents, peer pressure will become an even more powerful force in their lives.

I might add here that frequently loyalties and friendships among the typical adolescent drug experimenters are very warm and genuine. Too often a young person who doesn't fit anywhere else can find an accepting group here, and may be attracted to the group simply because it is so open.

3. *The battle for self-image.*

All of us also have within us the need to feel good about ourselves. We need to feel pleased with our past achievements and confident of future achievements. Most young people don't have as many sources of positive feedback as adults, so they measure their success in life by their success in relationships. Thus, when they are confronted with setbacks, they often try to escape the reality of their perceived failure in whatever ways are available to them.

Such "setbacks" don't have to be things you might consider major. Sometimes young people feel like failures when their grades are lower than they expected, when they aren't performing on the basketball court as well as they think they should, when they don't get a part in a play, when their homework doesn't satisfy them, when they aren't as beautiful as they would like to be, when they aren't growing as fast as they would like, and so forth.

4. *The need for a risk.*

As adults, we probably don't identify with this need as much as with some of the previous ones, but most adolescents do have some need for living life on the edge, for taking a chance, for doing something unusual—if for no other reason than the shock effect. Since drugs are so common, and since the whole anti-drug campaign assures us that there is a risk involved, some people fulfill their need for risk by experimenting with drugs.

5. *The need to experiment with adult behavior.*

At some point in his life, every adolescent says, "Look at me. I look adult. I am as big as an adult. Sometimes I am expected to act like an adult. I wonder how it feels to do some of the things adults do." If at this point young people know adult role models who use drugs, they may choose to experiment themselves.

A Parent's Response

Now that we accept the fact that drugs are common and that young people do have strong urges to experiment, what do we as parents do? What actions if any should we take?

1. *Provide a warm, loving, stable relationship.*

Give your child something he can depend on, no matter what happens. Does this sound like a replay of the rest of the book? No matter. It is just as important here, if not more so. Drug prevention begins and ends at home. You cannot assure your children that they will succeed in friendships. You cannot assure them that they will succeed in schoolwork, athletics, or whatever pursuit is so important. But you can assure them that they are successes as your children and that they bring you lots of happiness.

Frequently parents ask, "How will I know if my child gets into drugs?" This is a tough question which demands an honest and thorough answer, but the answer is similar to the challenge in the paragraph above. You must have a close enough relationship with your child that you will very quickly notice any changes in behavior or personality—especially if you are frightened by drugs.

Sometimes the drug experimenter becomes quieter, wants to spend time alone, becomes defensive, rebellious, or even paranoid. These changes are not definite threats of drug experimentation, but they are always suggestions. Know your child well enough to know when something is bothering him and if he is responding differently.

2. *Make sure your child knows the facts about drug usage.*

In recent years, most schools have implemented programs and curricula to address this task. Some of those programs are quite effective. I would encourage you to know what your school is doing in this area. Go to school and chat with the teacher. Take a look at some of the material. Talk to your child about what he is learning, and how he is processing it.

If your school doesn't have such a program to provide information, you can either take on this responsibility for your own child (you can order excellent materials from various sources) or you can get behind your school officials to implement something. I am convinced that every student in America needs to have the facts about drug usage, regardless of where he goes to school.

3. *Make sure your child knows your value structure.*

Children need to know what their parents believe. More importantly, they need to know what value precepts produce your actions. Make it easy for your children. Sit them down and tell them. If you have biblical principles which give your life direction and help in the face of pressure and crisis, don't cheat your children out of discovering the same source of direction. Teach them. For lessons this vital, don't trust the Sunday School teachers or the youth ministers.

4. *Teach your child how to make decisions.*

At the moment when the choice comes for your child, will he have any definite preplanned system to help him make a wise decision? Remember that at this moment he is going to have some pressure to act irrationally. Any rational decision will have to have been thought through ahead of time.

You can help your child here by teaching him to develop a system for making rational decisions on the spur of the moment. Since you go through the process every day, you should have some procedure in mind. Many school drug prevention programs are emphasizing this very ideal. In fact, some programs don't even speak of drugs as much as they teach a decision-making process.

5. *Cooperate with school officials.*

Teachers and administrators don't want your child using drugs either. Some schools have trained personnel in this area who have been a big help.

6. *Provide a warm, loving, stable relationship.*

I know this is a repeat of #1 on this list. I know I've said this before. But since this is the key, I will mention it again. This is the answer. If you want your child to stay away from the drug culture, make sure he feels accepted at home. Pray for your child on a regular basis. Claim the help of God, and make your child aware of your constant love.

Teenage Sex

Nature and culture unite in a conspiracy against adolescents. Nature equips them with the desires and functions of human sexuality. Culture restricts their use of those functions.

In many other cultures, people assume the responsibilities of adulthood in their teens. They become productive members of society. They marry and reproduce. But the American culture discourages this kind of early maturation. We delay the process until the young person graduates from high school or college. This makes sense within our culture. In the meantime, however, many adolescents are confused about what to do with their sexual desires.

Many don't survive the conflict. Nationwide polls frequently shock us with exact percentages. A survey taken in 1979 indicated that more than one-half of the nation's teenagers engaged in premarital sex. Regardless of what you think of statistics, the numbers do prove one point: Your child is probably not as naive as you think. If his classmates are figuring into the statistics, he has to be aware of the activity.

This is another tough lesson of parenthood. Sexuality is a difficult topic, and most of us prefer to avoid discussing it with our children. By so doing, we leave them open to seek education from the culture itself.

Through the medium of sex-appeal advertising, locker-room talk, and pornographic material, culture teaches our children that sex is dirty, mature, mysterious, desirable, clandestine, never innocent, animalistic, and sensually rewarding. If young people are going to get a different picture, someone will have to provide it.

Whether we like it or not, the only people who seem to be interested in accepting that challenge are the schools. I am not convinced that they are happy with the responsibility, but adolescent sexuality presents them with major problems. Teenage pregnancy, venereal diseases, the threat of AIDS, and even promiscuity are a blight on our educational system as well as on society as a whole.

For this reason, schools have almost been forced into taking action, so they have organized educational programs which attempt to teach the facts of human sexuality. Some elementary schools are providing third and fourth graders with information about their bodies through the use of films and sessions with the school nurse. Several middle schools have even more thorough sessions with several weeks of lessons concerning all aspects of sexual behavior. High school biology classes frequently include at least one unit on the human body which naturally covers sexual capabilities and reproduction.

For all of this, these school programs are caught up in questions and controversy. Where do they get material? What approach are they going to use—a very conservative one or a more liberal approach which says that sex is all right as long as you don't get pregnant or contract a disease? Who is going to teach the class, and what is that person's sexual orientation?

These are important questions that should be asked of every school program. If you know that your child is involved in any kind of sex education program at school, I would recommend that you go to the school and ask politely to look at the material. For issues this important, you need to know what your child is studying.

If you don't like the tone or the philosophy of the materials being used, be prepared to suggest alternatives. (You may have to do your homework.) Get acquainted with the teacher. Let him know how you feel about this important subject.

But after you have done all this, remind yourself that all of these school programs have an inherent limitation which will never sufficiently teach your child everything he needs to know. School programs will always have to focus primarily on the facts of human sexuality. They can never comprehensively or effectively deal with the emotions or with the spirituality of this gift that God has given us.

That is your job. How I shudder to have to say that, but it is true. And truth is very important in this area. Not long ago a church friend of mine complained about the sex education program at the local elementary school. "I take care of all that business at home," he assured me.

"Oh good," I said. "I'm so glad to hear that. I know of twenty-five sets of parents at our church who need some instruction on how to handle this. Call me and let's set up a seminar for you to teach us." My friend never called back.

I don't blame him. I am frightened of this topic too, particularly when it comes to teaching my own child. But parents must take this responsibility. The issue is too vital. The problems are too real. Our children do experience sexual urges and temptations. They do get an assortment of teaching about what the whole process means. And they do need some help to get it all straight.

Whether you want to admit it or not, your adolescent child is a sexual being who has been given a precious gift and potential. He has a body which is, in the words of Paul, a temple of the Holy Spirit. He will need some instruction in how to offer it to God.

Alcohol

Although alcohol is a drug—actually, the most abused drug in this country—I have chosen to treat it in a separate section because schools and society treat it differently. As I pointed out earlier, in recent years drug usage has appeared to lose its appeal to many of our young people. It is no longer "cool" to take drugs. But this isn't the case with alcohol. As the use of other drugs has diminished, teenage alcohol consumption has increased.

Recently, I asked a student his estimate of drug users in his suburban high school. He reported, "No more than twenty percent." I then asked his estimate of alcohol users. He reported, "More than seventy percent."

For the adolescent, alcohol is more readily available and is more socially acceptable. But it is still a drug and needs to be treated as one.

While scientists are still trying to document the dangers of some drugs, we already know the dangers of alcohol. There is no mystery here. There is no need for us to try to deceive ourselves. Teenage alcoholism is a reality. We cannot afford to take a soft stand on this problem simply because society is willing to treat it differently than any other drug problem.

Since I do equate alcohol with other forms of drugs, I begin this discussion with the same presupposition—that for the teenager, consumption in any amount is dangerous. I realize my viewpoint may be an old-fashioned notion, and this observation may in itself be part of the problem. These days there are few models of total abstinence in a child's life.

The adolescent years are at best tenuous and precarious. I just don't see the wisdom of a young person's adding further risk by dulling his judgment with drink. There are too many adverse possibilities—reduced academic performance, alcoholism, and, when your child gets older, automobile accidents. Any young person who deals with alcohol runs the risk of damaging his life.

Presently, the temptations to drink are somewhat different from the temptations to experiment with other forms of drugs. Many students' adult models, who strongly denounce drugs with appropriate fear and trembling, do drink and advertise the fact. For the young person, drinking becomes a symbol of romantic and exciting adult behavior.

There is also something rather romantic in taking a chance and living through it to tell about it. In the halls of any high school, there is no greater hero than a sixteen year old with a newly won speeding ticket. Crowds gather rapidly and demand a blow-by-blow account of the whole ordeal. Even vicariously, those young people are thrilled with the excitement of chance. They want to take a risk, but a safe one.

Alcohol is perceived to be a safe risk. Young people know there is something tantalizingly dangerous about drinking, but they perceive it must not be too dangerous because they know sane, successful adults who apparently have not been hurt by occasional nipping. Of course, this risk taking is essential to peer acceptance. No one wants a friend who is unimaginative, bland, or cautious. So the young person proves his social worthiness by participating in the risk.

A Parent's Defense

As a parent, what is your defense against this? The answer is rather obvious. If you don't want your child to drink, you must present him with an adult model who is cheerful and fulfilled without any attachment to the deadening effect of alcohol. This model must be credible enough to convince the adolescent that the thrill doesn't justify the risk—that, in fact, the risk is greater than most adolescents think. You can tell your child all the facts. But if you want him to believe them, you have to *show* him. There is no other way. But while you are showing your child this powerful model, remember three things.

First, *don't forget his need to experiment with adult behavior and his need to take some risks.* The solution to something as profound and frightening as adolescent drinking might be as simple as your allowing him to participate in adult conversations when your friends come to visit. How good is he in adult conversation? Can he carry his own, or must he learn about being an adult from his adolescent friends? This is important enough for you to invest some time in further thought.

Second, *permit your adolescent to be an adolescent*. I don't find this advice at all inconsistent with the above paragraph. Let your child experiment with adult behavior. At the same time, permit him some thrills, some excitement, and enough risk to make him socially attractive. If you think going out for football is too dangerous for your child, make sure you have a substitute that will fulfill his inherent need to take risks. His choice might be a drinking spree.

Third, *your child should understand the value of his own body*. It's up to you to teach him. Some Scripture would also be helpful to support your ideas in this area.

I realize that these suggestions to curb the temptations of drinking in adolescents might seem superficial, but I am ready to defend them. There is a difference between the temptations of hard drugs and the temptations of alcohol. I suggest that you investigate the quality of the message of your child's role models as well as his perception of the risk.

A Question of Values

Despite the frightening tone, despite the various suggestions and warnings, despite the obvious complexity of the problem, the thrust of this whole chapter can be reduced to two questions: (1) What does your child value? and (2) Where has he established his uncrossable boundaries?

Keep in mind that we're talking about his own boundaries and not your boundaries for him. Those are boundaries which he must have in place before temptations come. And those boundaries must be strong enough to hold against the forces of peer pressure, the desire to rebel against parents, and the need for youthful experimentation.

Your child probably established his boundaries after listening to and watching the authority figures in his life. Logically, we conclude that if you want his boundaries to be the same as yours, you must earn the right to be one of these authority figures who carry some power in his value formation. To earn that right, you must relate to your child, which takes us back to the thesis of this book.

Your ability to help your child survive and thrive in his world of school, home, friends, activities, and temptations depends on your personal relationship with him. It is easy for me to make that suggestion. It is always easier to talk about being a parent than it is to be one.

Homework Assignments for Parents

1. Is your relationship with your child strong enough to tell if he were considering involvement with drugs, sex, or alcohol? Have you sat down with him and discussed these "big three" areas?

2. Does your child talk to you about which people at school are actively involved in these harmful activities? How can you encourage him to be more open?

3. Is your child aware of why you choose not to get involved in habits that are harmful to your body? If not, what common-sense reasons can you give him that might be helpful when he encounters temptations to try these things out?

4. What would you do if you discovered your child was taking drugs? Or sexually active? Or drinking every weekend? How would you handle these situations?

A FINAL WORD

12

Working with the Institution of School

Throughout this book, I have addressed the question of how you can help your child survive and thrive in school by focusing the discussion and suggestions on the personal or more direct perspective. I have tried to anticipate what your child might be encountering, and I have tried to suggest ways for you to help him meet the challenges of being young.

In keeping with this perspective, I have proposed that you analyze and support schools by concentrating your efforts on the individual classroom teacher—that you know what is going on in your child's classroom, that you know how your child is responding to what is going on, that you stay close enough to your child to know the strengths and weaknesses of his school experience, and that you and the rest of your family are prepared to fill in the gaps in your child's education.

As a veteran educator, I am happy with this focus. After my twenty years in the profession, I have concluded that each student responds to the giant institution of school in his own unique way. For some students, school is a positive institution. For some, it is negative, perhaps even destructive. From this, I have further concluded that any significant change in the quality of education will begin in individual classrooms with individual teachers.

But at the same time, I realize the inadequacy of this simple approach. School is a giant, impersonal, sometimes corrupt, sometimes unwieldy institution. It would be foolish for me to suggest that you don't need to be interested in the institution itself. Unless you have a legal alternative, your child will have to spend a minimum of 14,000 hours of his life there.

Wise parents know their children. They know what is happening to their children in the classroom. *Thorough* parents also know something about the institution of school. This takes some study, so I conclude the book with this chapter introducing you to some of the present concerns of those people charged with the task of directing the institution.

Let me emphasize the word *introduce*. Actually, I am only going to mention some concerns. In this short space, I will not present enough information for you to make a decision about any one of them. However, I would like to stimulate your interest.

I do have one note of caution. If you decide to be a school reformer—carry banners, publish material, lead parades, plan demonstrations, disrupt the school board meeting, beat on administrators' doors—do it for the right reasons. Make sure that in all your efforts to make the world a better place, your primary motive is to help your own child. Don't make the mistake of getting so wrapped up in provoking change that you forget to talk to your child, help him read, watch him play sports or music, and host his friends. In other words, don't forget to be a parent.

A Matter of Politics

I enjoy walking past elementary schools when students are dismissed in the afternoon. I like to watch the children and listen to their spontaneous, serious conversations. During these moments, I see purity and innocence, fervor and excitement, logic and immaturity. But I am shocked back into reality when I remember that frequently decisions affecting the quality of these young lives are made by cigar-chomping, foot-stomping, hand-banging, wheeling-dealing politicians. There is something incongruous between the innocence of the playground and the maneuvering and compromise of the smoke-filled committee rooms. But that is the way it is.

Politicians decide whether those children walk to school or ride the bus. They decide what courses the children take, how many classmates they have, what college courses the teacher took, and what the children can and cannot buy to eat during school hours.

Remember, I am not evaluating this. I am simply mentioning it to point out that most decisions affecting school life are political decisions, and germinate and grow like other political decisions. Voters create noise. Politicians—after appropriate argument, consideration, and compromise—respond and produce a new school law that requires your child to take physical education each day or prevents him from buying potato chips. This is how the system works.

I emphasize this to remind you that if you want to effect change, you must be prepared to fight political battles. But you can, in fact, win. Many people just like you have won.

One winter, I had to drive on a famous national highway each morning on my way to work. I began to notice the small children walking along that busy, dangerous highway on their way to school. I also noticed that buses with empty seats whizzed right past those children. That didn't seem right to me, so in a moment of unusual civic nobility, I decided to investigate.

I went to the principal, and he explained the state law. The school could legally transport children who lived more than one and a half miles from the building. In fact, that state would give the district money to transport those children. But the state wouldn't pay for students who lived within a mile and a half; thus the walkers.

The principal was kind enough. He even pulled out the giant school code, blew the dust off, and let me read the law myself. I believed the principal, but I could tell that I wasn't going to accomplish anything here. The issue was bigger than local school policy.

By then, I was so charged with the joy of civic duty that I decided to carry the issue further. I convinced the local newspaper editor to get involved. He took some pictures of those buses whizzing by the children, and he wrote some persuasive editorials. Parents began to respond. There was a letter campaign to state legislators. Before spring came, there was a rider attached to the state law that said the state would pay for transporting a child who lived within a mile and a half if the child's route to school was dangerous. Since the highway in question is as dangerous as it is famous, those children started riding the bus.

I don't take the credit for this rider, but I want you to see how the process works. I want you to have confidence that it *does* work, and it works when intelligent people like you make it work.

Great Debates

Let me list four of the issues which are presently requiring political debate and subsequent decisions. You may get excited about one or more of these.

1. *School Finances*

If your school is typical, it is in financial trouble. The reason for financial trouble is simple:

Costs have gone up more rapidly than income. The solution to the financial woes is to find more income or reduce the costs of education. (With such economic brilliance, I should be president.)

Despite what some people think, rising costs are not necessarily the result of increased waste. Inflation has hit the school budget. During one school year in the last decade, the cost of paper tripled. Schools buy gasoline at the same price that you do. During the last ten years, cost-of-living raises in salaries have literally destroyed school budgeting theory. Salaries now take as much as twenty-five percent more of the school budget than they did ten years ago. Let me emphasize that these are *cost-of-living* raises. Teachers have no more buying power now than they did ten years ago.

One alternative solution to the financial difficulties is to find the money to meet these rising costs. There are two possibilities—raise taxes or charge the parents for some of the school's services.

Raising taxes is not a popular idea, particularly in states like California and Massachusetts where voters have recently passed propositions to freeze or lower local taxes. Apparently, these taxpayer revolts are going to spread to other states. If you have not already done so, in the near future you will probably have to make a decision about whether the schools in your area should have more money. Are you prepared to vote on that issue? Let's check with a short examination.

- *What kind of tax is used to finance your school?*
- *What is the annual per-pupil expenditure in your district?*
- *How much of that do you pay with your taxes?*
- *How much money does your school district receive from the state for every day your child is in school? (This is something you need to know before you plan that trip and pull your child out of school for a week.)*
- *What is the pay schedule for teachers in your district?*

If you have the answer to all (or even most) of those questions, you are now in a position to decide whether raising taxes is a possible solution to the financial problems in your district. If you don't, you shouldn't feel guilty. Most people, even the educators, wouldn't be able to answer all these questions. But I want to make the point that sometimes we are asked to vote on crucial issues even though we may not have as much information as we need.

The second possibility for meeting rising costs is to ask the parents to pay for some of the services. Some districts have already implemented this procedure. If parents want their children to have a band, the parents must help pay the band director. If parents want their children to play football, they must help pay for the program. I know of districts where this is working well. But it does seem to contradict the American principle of free, public education, and there may be legal problems if some parents protest.

The second alternative solution to the financial difficulty of schools is to cut educational costs, and this means to cut educational services. There are several possibilities such as:

- *Eliminate or reduce extracurricular activities.*
- *Eliminate special programs such as special education, programs for the gifted, and enriched courses with lower enrollment.*
- *Increase class size. (If an elementary school increased maximum class size from thirty to thirty-five, the school could reduce its staff by almost ten percent.)*
- *Close schools. (Packed buildings are more economically efficient.)*

It is easy for me to list these possibilities, but choosing one to implement is another matter. Yet someone has to make a decision. Your school board may be looking at such decisions right now. If so, those members need some suggestions from you. How important are the extracurricular activities to you and your child? Are you willing to give up your neighborhood building in order to keep art teachers in the elementary school? How should the school handle children with learning disabilities? (That question becomes even more important when your child is in this category.) If the class size increases, are you willing to make up for the loss of personal attention your child is going to suffer?

If your district is typical, these questions are relevant. The financial problem is a crucial one. Are you prepared to be a part of the solution?

2. *Teacher Organizations*

Teachers have had some kind of a national organization since shortly after the Civil War. Presently, there are two major choices—the American Federation of Teachers, which is a labor union, and the National Education Association, which is the historical professional association. Although both organizations like to enumerate their distinctions, for the taxpayer and parent they are more alike than different. Both are national umbrella organizations with state and local groups underneath. Both have made major contributions to improving the teaching profession. Both provide professional and personal services for their members.

But in recent years, the teacher organizations have assumed a new role in our society. In most states, teachers have won the right to collective bargaining or negotiation. In those states, teachers in a given district are represented by one of the two organizations. Local teachers have the power of organization behind them when they negotiate for higher salaries or better working conditions.

The process works about the same as it does in any other labor-management relationship. Labor presents a proposed contract; management presents an alternative; hassle follows. If an agreement is reached, school continues. If not, the teachers strike. It is all rather commonplace now.

But the procedure may not be as harmless as it appears on the surface. I am convinced that any labor-management dispute will eventually be reflected in the product. When a dispute occurs in the schools, that product is your child. We have not had the negotiation process long enough for us to determine the educational effects of bargaining and subsequent strikes, but there are some possible dangers that bear watching (without even mentioning the obvious problems that strikes create for students).

For one thing, collective bargaining has split the profession. There is definitely a "them and us" attitude between administrators and teachers. These people work in the same building, embrace the same goals and objectives, are paid from the same tax base, deal with the same children, eat in the same lunchroom, and smoke and complain in the same lounge. Yet they are divided at contract time.

I am perplexed. I am pleased with the improvements that the negotiation process has brought to the teaching profession, but I am also concerned about the possible dangers, the hurt, the scars that come from a split profession.

Is there some way that we could have the best of both worlds, improvement of the profession—the salary, the working conditions, the standards—without the injuries of division?

3. *Minimum Competency Testing*

Educators and consumers alike have become concerned with what is an apparent decrease in learning skills and educational competence. Experts (sometimes called researchers) have ventured guesses (sometimes called research) as to why Johnny can't read and Suzie can't cipher.

One possible suspect is an animal called social promotion—the idea that students are promoted from grade to grade simply because they have spent the appropriate number of hours in a given grade level. So we have students who are promoted into high school (and may even graduate) who can't read, write, or do arithmetic.

The obvious solution to this problem is to check the student's progress at various times during his academic career to see whether he has acquired the requisite tools. Educators all across the nation are now busy developing "minimum competency tests" to check to see if a student is fit to be promoted to the next level.

As I said earlier, this seems to be the obvious solution to a rather disturbing problem. But, as usual, implementing the theory has brought some controversy. Some parents claim that the tests are unfair because they are written with an ethnic or middle-class bias. Others maintain that if the student spends his time in school, he should receive the privileges reserved for graduates. If he didn't learn anything, the school is at fault and he shouldn't be punished.

Some educators claim that the tests will lead to poorer teaching instead of better. They maintain that teachers will become interested only in having their students learn enough to pass the test.

Let me remind you that my original purpose was to introduce you to these topics, and this is a very superficial introduction to this very complex problem. It does concern you, because your educators and your politicians are probably debating the question now.

I warn you that what you have read here does not make you competent to hold court at the PTA meeting, but recent literature has been filled with discussions of minimum competency and standardized testing. I encourage you to investigate further. Your state legislator may need your opinion soon.

4. *Text and Material Selection*

Notice how I saved the real controversy for last. This is currently a hot topic. I don't want to offend any segment of readers this near the end by taking an unpopular position, but this topic does provoke intense emotion from proponents of both sides. I am not afraid of that emotion. It is good to feel strongly about something. But neither group should let emotions crowd out common sense and reason when something as precious as our children are involved.

The question is actually a rather simple one. Who has the right to decide what materials students will study? Traditionally educators have made those decisions almost by themselves. Some schools have solicited advice from concerned parent groups, but the final decisions have usually been made by the educators.

In recent years, parents have demanded a stronger voice. These demands have come in various forms—speeches at board meetings, representation on textbook-selection committees, lawsuits, and even public demonstrations.

But while parents and educators wrestle over this problem, there is a question that must be answered first. Regardless of who selects the textbooks and other reading material, on what basis is that selection made? Do we choose books because of their quality without consideration of orthodoxy? Do we protect our children from confronting ideas, language, or emotions that might be controversial or offensive? What are the criteria for making such decisions?

The issue of text selection is a many-faceted one which must be approached with knowledge and wisdom. If you have a child in school, you have already made some commitment to the issue. If you have not been personally involved in textbook selection, you have in effect stated your opinion that you are willing to let educators make those choices. If you have been involved, then you have stated your opinion that parents deserve a voice.

If you want to make your opinions count, the place for you to begin is to learn how textbooks are selected in your district. Some states have a state-adoption committee which approves all instructional materials at the state level. In other states, such decisions are left to individual districts. In some of those districts, there is a district-wide committee. Sometimes the decisions are left entirely to the individual teacher. You will need to know who selects the texts for your child. If you are a person with common sense, you may need to get involved in the politics surrounding the textbook selections.

Involvement: Putting Information into Practice

The four issues discussed above are just a few out of many that concern the people who make the educational decisions affecting your child. By this brief introduction, I want to make several points. First, these are major concerns. They merit your attention. They are complex issues that deny simple answers. They are political issues. They concern you and your child. These issues need your response.

So what can you do? First, you can make yourself knowledgeable. Then you can put your knowledge to work. Several outlets exist for you to do so.

Attend a Parent Conference.

Perhaps the simplest and most overlooked form of parent involvement is to attend scheduled conferences with your child's teachers and counselors. If you get invited, make the effort to go. I predict that something valuable will come from the exchange.

Too many parents are threatened by those invitations to come to school. Don't let the invitations or the school personnel put you on the defensive. You have paid for a part of that school. You have a right to be there. If you have questions, ask them. If you have suggestions, make them. School personnel are plagued by lack of parent interest. Show the teacher that at least you are interested. It will make his day.

Become a Volunteer Teacher.

Once you get confident about visiting the teacher, you may want to volunteer a few hours each week to work at school. Many schools are using parent volunteers effectively in a variety of functions. You may listen to students read, help put up bulletin boards, or supervise the playground. But you will be doing important work, and you will be learning more about your child's school and what goes on in his life each day.

Consult the School Board.

When you become confident in the school building, you may want to start attending board meetings. Why don't you attend and find out what issues concern those officials elected to run your school? Better yet, why don't you attend to let those officials know that they can depend on you?

You don't need a special invitation or a ticket. Just call the local school and ask when the meeting is. The board can close the meeting during discussion of personnel, but when that occurs, someone will politely ask you to leave.

Most school boards have more work to do than they can get done. Remember that these people serve for no salary and have other careers themselves. Many boards rely on special task forces composed of interested private citizens. If you have attended board meetings a few times, you may be asked to serve. Serving in such a capacity will give you the opportunity to learn about the major issues and will let you see how decisions are made.

If you don't think your board is doing a good job, run for office yourself. Any legal voter is eligible. All you need is a small filing fee, time to campaign, and an acute interest in serving children. Don't excuse yourself on the grounds that you haven't been trained. Neither has anyone else. There are no special courses to take. Just get involved.

If you get elected, you may wish at times that you had surrendered your life to something easier, such as being a missionary to an isolated tribe in the Amazon Valley. School board members receive no monetary compensation and very few kind words. They are available to the public for advice (mostly unsolicited and not usable), and they are constantly criticized. Consequently many districts do not have their best talent on their school boards. I urge you to take up the cause yourself. If you don't see yourself in such a role, at least make some contribution to the mental well-being of those who do serve.

Consult Your Legislators.

You can also be a direct influence on state and federal law. Every congressman and every senator has a mailbox. Despite the rumors to the contrary, every one of them can read. Acquaint yourself with the issues. Think about the possible consequences of a piece of legislation. Then write your congressman. Your letter may be the soundest piece of advice he gets on that particular issue. Your message is important, and your insight, if it originates in the Spirit of the Living God, is precious. Make yourself heard.

Your Child: Where You and the School Meet

As you become involved at the school, district, state, or federal level, don't forget the principal character in all this effort—your child. Despite all your other accomplishments and all the other great contributions you are making to the history of humankind, your child is the one contribution that will most nearly represent what you have lived for. Such a significant contribution deserves your time, your study, your attention, and your best effort.

You are not alone in this endeavor of bringing your child through the pitfalls and promises of childhood to meaningful adulthood. You must entrust some of that responsibility to the school and to society itself. Your role as a parent is to coordinate all the child's experiences into one unified, consistent, teaching agent.

Parenthood would be a less frustrating, if not easier, enterprise if we could just control what our children encounter. But since we can't eliminate all the negative and harmful influences, we must settle for the task of coordinating.

While your child is in school, he will be under the direct supervision and influence of more than forty different adult authorities. During that time, he will also be subjected to the power of scores of his peers. Obviously, some of these people are going to contradict your suggestions. Some will contradict each other. Some will contradict your child's own value and knowledge systems.

But these contradictions won't do much damage as long as your child has a stable, consistent, understanding, sensitive touchstone to help him evaluate, integrate, and unify these diverse sources and experiences. That's what parents are for, to be that touchstone, to have a close enough relationship with their child to provide stability in his life.

After having studied the educational scene firsthand for all these years, I am convinced that your child can survive and even thrive in school. Thousands do. Although he might even make it by himself, it would be easier for him if he doesn't have to tackle the task alone.

As you get involved, you may make some lifelong friends. You may discover some dedicated, loving people. You may find some professionals who need your sympathy and concern. You may even find an ally to help you combat the hairstyles on your child that you don't approve of.

And who knows, helping your son or daughter through the mysteries of school and school relationships might become some of the most memorable and rewarding moments of parenthood. Try it and see.

Homework Assignments for Parents

1. Imagine your child's school were to have an immediate financial crisis that threatened to be long-term. What course of action would you recommend?

2. How aware are you of the materials your child is receiving at school? Are you allowed input in determining your child's textbooks? What changes would you make, if any, if it were up to you to select such materials?

3. At this point, do you have any unanswered questions about your child's school? If so, find out where you can get the answers and then go talk to the appropriate people.